TO FIND

The Search for Meaning in Life on The Gringo Trail

— a memoir —

J. R. Klein

Publisher: Del Gato
Editors: Nick May, Hunter Atherton
Library of Congress Control Number: 2019915655
ISBN: 978-1-7339069-5-1
ISBN: 978-1-7339069-4-4 (ebook)

DEDICATION

To Jeanne

And to everyone I met, every experience I had, and everything I
learned on The Gringo Trail

Also by J. R. Klein

Frankie Jones
A Distant Past, An Uncertain Future
The Ostermann House

ACKNOWLEDGMENTS

A big thanks to the Del Mar Danish Pastry Shop, which is now long gone but used to be on Camino Del Mar in Del Mar, California. It was there that each day under the eucalyptus trees I scribbled down the words from the ragged pages of the diary that I carried on the Gringo Trail and turned them into the current memoir. A nod also goes out to the simple Smith-Corona typewriter and subsequently to the WordStar program I used on my first computer to transcribe my hand-written notes. Most of this was written when the events described in the book were fresh in my mind. And yet, as I think about them now, they could easily have taken place just yesterday.

PROLOGUE

This book is a memoir of my travels through Mexico and Central America in the early 1980s. As you read through, if you come across descriptions of places and islands with which you are familiar, and you find yourself saying, 'That's outright garbage. I've been there and what is being described is nothing like what I know', ask yourself when it was that you were there. In 1980, most of the coastal islands from the tip of the Yucatan down to Belize were virtually uninhabited, very much the way they are described here. There were no high-rise hotels, no resorts, no casinos—barely any accommodations at all. Life was quiet, simple, and beautiful, so long as a dreaded hurricane did not pay a visit. It was possible to live cheaply and travel cheaply back then. My total daily expenses ran less than five dollars a day for transportation, lodging, and food combined.

The islands as described in the book are gone now. That is to say, the islands of course are still there, but they are not the same today as they were back then. Whether that's a good thing or not is for each of us to decide.

Finally, the names of some of the people in the book have been changed—principally that of myself and Stefan Kale and a few other people. Most have remained as they were in life.

J. R. Klein — 2019

Somewhere on the Gringo Trail the world will change—an old sun will set and a new one will rise. After that, all meaning loses meaning; all life takes on new life. The world will turn a little differently. It will become both bigger and smaller. The blood in your veins will singe your soul in the quest for life, and your heart will be ransomed to love.

— from Miles

Part One

THE DESERT

CHAPTER ONE

June 2, 1980 – Day 1

I can never remember being as bored as I was in the spring of 1980. Nothing in my life was good; nothing was bad. Nothing was right; nothing was wrong. I had no money, but I was not broke. I had no job, but I was not unemployed. I had a lover, but I wasn't in love. I was healthy, though I didn't know it. I had just finished a doctoral degree. Drained, weary, and empty, living in Baltimore, unmotivated and unhappy. My life seemed stalled. Back then the only shred of life and energy and excitement came from the moments spent with Stefan Kale—photographer, artist, friend.

Stef understood everything I told him about my life and the people who jockeyed it in the unholy human way people have of doing such things. All winter and spring I had spent at Stef's apartment in the evenings after leaving the university. Instead of going home and submerging myself in hours of studying and thinking and reading, instead, as if lured into the night like a teenager drawn to the streets, I went to Bolton Hill and crossed over to Lanvale Street.

And so on those cold still nights when snow piled high on the window ledge in pure silvery mounds, and the radiator worked hard, bang-clang all night, when there was little else to do but fantasize about such wonderful things as sunshine and freedom—yes, freedom from the endless drudgery of graduate school—there I would sit for hours, until morning at times, talking to Stef or watching him work in the darkroom. Working negatives again and again slowly and deliberately until each had been printed perfectly. Wonderful black and white photographs bought and sold in a half dozen galleries from Baltimore to New York.

One evening late in May, I said, "I don't know, Stef. I feel like I'm wasting my time. I'm completely burned out. I've been thinking about…well…I've been thinking about quitting science. Maybe it isn't right for me. I don't know."

No one could understand this better than Stef. Always ready to pick up and leave, to abandon the world, to vanish from existence on some forgotten corner of the planet. Vagabond with camera in hand.

For me, though, this was more than a desultory escape. Its roots ran deep into the marrow of my existence. I knew the feeling, had felt it growing inside me. Like a ghoul after my soul, it had been haunting me for a long time, carrying with it the saddening doubt that comes from making a decision with great certainty only to have it turned sadly and meanly against you. A nasty trick you've played on yourself, believing you knew what you wanted and then being confronted with the reality of your mistake. The necessity of leaving behind nearly four years of hard work and walking away empty handed. You drag out the decision until the inevitable becomes a slow gasping death. And now only one thing was crystal clear to me—it was time to leave. The sooner, the farther away, the better.

On that drizzly night, we again ran through the list of where to go, as we had done a thousand times before. Canada. Too close, too much like the US. Europe was rejected due to the cost needed to get us there and back. What's more, Europe—saturated with remnants of its creative and intellectual genius gloatingly displayed across cathedral ceilings—was far too cerebral for my fragile mental state. Not at all what I needed right now. Africa had a grand connotation. But it, too, was far away and costly. India, Pakistan, Sri Lanka, Borneo, New Guinea and a dozen other places in the Far East were beyond the limits of my pocketbook.

We left the apartment and angled down Lanvale Street past the Maryland Institute of Art. The night air was cool and moist. Up above, light from a red sky filtered through leafy trees. We walked for a block until we arrived at The Eutaw Street Tavern— The Eutaw as it was known. Meeting place for Institute people, would-be artists, local drunks, and us.

Stef ordered beer from Chuck, who was a good bartender and always talked to us when we came in. Chuck, being a pretty decent artist in his own right, though lacking any drive for recognition or success (and anyway, bartending paid the rent) could talk about anything. Football, baseball, art, politics, sex—anything.

Chuck set two pints on the counter—white foamy heads bubbled to the top. Stef leaned against the cracked bar and drew in a long slug of beer. Chuck looked at me and saw the sadness in my exhausted eyes and pulled three shot glasses from the shelf and filled them with rye and winked. We all knocked back the liquor.

A student from the Institute walked up. She stood behind Stef and rested her hands on his shoulders. She wore jeans and a cotton top, some sort of faded tie-dyed affair. This person, Laurie was her name, I'd seen many times when we were in The Eutaw. In a soft, low, sexy voice she said, "Well, my, my, my, if it *isn't* Stefan Kale. So tell me, what brings the great Stefan Kale into our humble little bar?"

Stef turned and gave Laurie a trivial smile.

I watched as Laurie swayed to the music that flowed from the jukebox. She projected a carefreeness that pulled at my psyche now more so than ever, all of which allowed me to momentarily forget the misery of higher education. There was always something about Laurie I liked, though the total extent of our conversation usually went something like this: "Hi, Alex, seen Stef?"

"Got any plans?" Laurie said to Stef.

Stef worked on his pint. "Heading out. Going away with Alex here. You know Alex, don't you?"

Laurie glanced over, puckered her lips, feigned a kiss, and returned to Stef. "Really. So where are you going?"

Now caught without an explanation, Stef reached for his beer, and with that he purchased time while searching for an answer. It really didn't matter. I mean, he could have said anything—any place would do. What difference would it make to Laurie, or to us for that matter as we stood in The Eutaw drinking beer? But then in some instinctual sort of way, Stef said, "Well...well, Laurie, we're going, uh…we're going far away."

Laurie waited for Stef's eventual pronouncement, tapping her fingers on the bar to the music all the while.

"That's right, you see we're going to…to Central America, that's where."

When Stef said that, it was as if the music quit blasting from the jukebox and the tavern turned into an empty tomb. Nothing but long slow silence. Stef had said it. That fast—that quickly—it was done. He had found our spot, our place, our destiny, our journey. We were going to Central America.

It had begun.

CHAPTER TWO

June 3, 1980 – Day 2

The next day I went straight to Johns Hopkins University and trudged down the long corridor of Shuler Hall, foggy headed and probably reeking of ketones from my late night at The Eutaw, having been fed countless shots of rye from Chuck. Shoulders drooping, I walked into the office of my PhD advisor, Dr. Ned Markham, professor of biophysics. He looked up at me and returned to the work on his desk.

"What's up, Alex?" he said in a voice I'd heard a thousand times.

I waited a second and then dropped the bomb. I told him I was leaving science. An abrupt stillness fell across the room for what seemed like a near eternity. He leaned back in his chair and stared at me and shook his head, flummoxed. "Leaving science…what do you mean you're leaving science? You have a tremendous postdoctoral fellowship waiting for you at MIT in Boston. What about that? It's a great lab. One of the best in the world. Think of what you'll learn." Markham set his pencil down softly. "Why, Alex?"

"I don't know, Ned, zero motivation anymore," I replied,

apologetically. I tried to explain my feelings, the lack of enthusiasm for my experiments, the drudgery that greeted me every time I thought of reading one more research paper, cracking one more book, deriving one more equation, packing one more fact into an already clogged brain. I was not exploring the vast unknowns of science. I was digging ditches.

Markham leaned forward, neck craned, brow furrowed as if he had missed something in all this. He pulled in a long, deep breath and exhaled. "Now look, Alex," he said, arms held forth like Carl Sagan about to describe the workings of the universe. "Look…I know how it is. You busted your ass to finish your PhD, and it seemed endless, I know. But you did, you finished. And now your whole life lies ahead."

I listened numbly.

"Have a seat," Markham said.

I slipped into a chair—a chair I practically owned. I had sat in it an infinite number of times when we kicked experiments around, brain-stormed ideas together, conjured up new approaches and techniques for the lab. Sitting there letting my mind go wild was once cherished time for me. When I would dump a crazy idea on Markham, he would get up and walk to the window and stare out across the upper quad at the red Georgian buildings of Homewood Campus. He'd stand there a long time thinking, then he would turn and say, "Hmm…maybe. Let's let this ferment a while." It was one of his favorite phrases. He'd come back in a day or two with the verdict: "All right, Alex, give it a whirl" or "Won't work," and he would proceed through the details on the blackboard as to why my idea was doomed from the get-go. There was once a time when I loved those moments.

"What's happened is that you hit the hill, that's all," Markham said. "It happens to everyone…heartbreak hill, I mean. You know what heartbreak hill is, Alex, don't you?"

I nodded.

"Boston Marathon. Mile twenty. You look at the hill and say, I can't do it. I'll never make it up that. But you do. You know how? You lean into it. You look straight ahead and lean into it. That's how. For some people it happens when they're in graduate school…the hill I mean. For others, it comes later. Like for you. It's common, Alex, really common."

The analogy didn't resonate. I wasn't trying to slog my way up some hill in a grueling race. I had been doing that every day for years now. And even if I succeeded, then what? Would my whole life become one gigantic torturous marathon, each day waking to another heartbreak hill? Here I was at Johns Hopkins University, and all I could think about was finding a way to end what I had worked so hard for.

Markham got out of his chair. He walked to the window and stared out for a long while. He was not contemplating experiments this time. He came back and lowered himself into his chair and looked at me with the saddest eyes I had ever seen, at a loss for words, out of ammunition. Rare for him.

"So what are you going to do?" he finally uttered.

I explained my plans.

"You're *not* serious," he said, quietly and intently.

I nodded bashfully.

"And what about MIT?"

"I'll get in touch with them."

"Oh, geez, Alex…Central America?" he said, rubbing his forehead. "They're having revolutions down there. You know that, don't you? Nicaragua, El Salvador, Honduras, even Mexico. My God, it's a mess."

I wasn't going there for those reasons, I told him.

"How long are you going to be gone?"

I shook my head.

Markham sighed. "So when are you leaving?"

"Soon…right away almost."

"Maybe you should go home and think about this for a while."

"I have, Ned."

"Take as much time as you need."

"It won't do any good."

"A week, two weeks, three weeks. It doesn't matter. As much time as you need."

I couldn't answer.

Markham toyed with his pencil. He drummed the tips of his fingers on his desk and looked out the window. Turning back to me, he nodded blankly and gasped softly. "All right…all right, if that's what you want," came his reply. "I don't know what to say. I still think…well…well drop a card and tell us where you are from time to time, huh?"

"I will…I will, Ned." After what seemed like a long dreadful pause, I pulled myself from the chair and walked to the door, then turned and said, "Ned, uh, thanks for all the…for the—" I couldn't finish the sentence. I walked down the hall and out the building, refusing to look back.

I informed Skeets, my roommate, and Maureen, my girl-friend, of my plans. Maureen went completely nuts. I was going to Central America with that *insanely* mad photographer friend of mine?

"Oh, *Jesus*, Alex, you've gone totally off the deep end this time. Totally! What's gotten into you!" She looked into my hollow eyes, sighed heartily, and said, "Alex." The word fell deftly from her lips. "What you need to do is get back to your plans. What about Boston? What about us? We were going together…remember? My job here sucks and…and when did you decide this anyway?"

"A long time ago actually."

"You never said a word."

"I wanted to be sure. It's a big…you know—"

Maureen threw her hands in the air. She walked across the room, turned, and said, "Christ, you've just given up. Flat out quit."

She was right, I had given up. But it didn't matter. I could no longer continue on. I could no longer plan my life a month at a time, a week at a time, a day at a time. I had to leave. I needed to disconnect myself from the clock of life.

"Is this the end of us? Is that what you're saying?" she asked, faintly.

I didn't answer immediately. "Everything between us is the same," I finally said.

Maureen rolled her eyes. "The same?" she muttered. "The

same? And you're heading off with crazy Stef to where? To Central America somewhere? Is that it?"

"It's not about that. Don't you see? It's about my life, my career. Stef or no Stef. Central America or no Central America."

She looked straight at me. "Are you coming back?"

"Of course," I answered, instantly. Though I could not say it in true honesty, it was the reply I wanted her to hear—the reply I wanted myself to hear.

⋏

I purchased a simple rucksack from an Army-Navy store and constructed a bedroll out of an old army blanket and a strip of foam rubber. After all, how cold could it get in the deserts and tropics, right? Stef had a tent and some cooking utensils. I prepared a small medical kit with bandages and gauze, sutures and needles, scissors, tourniquets, antihistamine and epinephrine for insect stings and allergic reactions, and syringes, and got a friend at the medical school to write a letter stating we were both thoroughly experienced with everything in the kit. This, we hoped, would ward off wanton accusations of drug trafficking by the ever-probing Federales.

I pulled together every nickel, every penny, I could gather. It came to a grand total of just under five hundred dollars: two hundred and fifty to start with, and another two hundred and forty from my last fellowship check that Skeets would wire to me at some as-yet-undetermined point in Central America. How long would it last? I couldn't say. At a dollar or two a day, I could stretch it for six months or more. After that, I had no idea. But a small price to pay to set my mind free, to unfurl my spirit, to un-shackle my compressed psyche—it was a bargain at any cost.

We needed a cheap, fast way to get to the border of Mexico. I spent one afternoon on the phone calling around Baltimore and eventually located a car delivery agency. We could drive one to Texas, the man told me. "Sometime around the beginning of June."

Two days later we heard the good news. A car was waiting for us. We were to drive it to Fort Worth. This was it. We would leave today. I told Stef I'd pick up the car. He said he'd meet me at my place in an hour.

I took the bus to the office of the automobile company, where I deposited a hundred dollars and was given the keys to a pale green 1971 Ford Pinto and an address in Fort Worth, Texas. We had seven days to get there and were not to drive between 10 pm and 6 am. I gleefully signed the papers and drove off.

When I returned to Skeet's place, Stef was his usual buoyant self, lolling on the front porch like a summer cat basking in the warm June sun. Next to him was his pack, plump and full and ready—as well put together as an orange. Everything was in place. The pockets on the sides were neat and round and the pack was square and tight. His cameras were stashed safely inside. There was not a pinch of extra space.

Stef leaped from the porch and inspected the car inside and out. He walked around it again and again. I felt like a proud father bringing home the new family car. Stef sat behind the wheel and opened the glove compartment and then opened the hood and looked at the engine. He kicked the tires and beeped the horn and blared the radio and said, "Well, dammit, Alex, she's a beauty…a real beauty!"

We loaded our packs and climbed aboard. Just as we were ready to leave, I told Stef to wait, saying I'd be back in a minute. I went inside and climbed the stairs to the attic where I had stored what little I owned. Pulling out a book by Thoreau, I scribbled down the words:

> *I went to the woods because I wished to live deliberately,*
> *to front only the essential facts of life, and see if I could*
> *not learn what it had to teach, and not, when I came to*
> *die, discover that I had not lived.*

Maybe I wasn't going into the woods as Thoreau knew it, but those few words described everything I was feeling. Neatly folding the paper, I stuck it into my wallet.

Stef took to the wheel and aimed the car south onto the Baltimore beltway and then onto I-95, which would carry us past Washington, DC, down through Virginia, across the great collage of southern states under the wide belly of America, and out to our destiny. I had no idea what lay ahead but it didn't matter, I did not want what lay behind.

CHAPTER THREE

June 5, 1980 – Day 4

Many times in my life I've driven long distances on the interstate. It's not the prettiest nor the most scenic way to travel, and there's a certain monotony that catches up with you on these roads, but the superhighway has its place. It is for man what air is to the bird. With it we glide across the land, turning in wide smooth arcs, rising and dipping in gentle swells as if on a current of air. When I'm on the highway, I get a strange sort of feeling that comes from being a spectator to the world around me, drugged by the hum of the wheels on the pavement blasting along at seventy miles an hour.

The Pinto whizzed down the highway past Washington DC and into the lush hills of Virginia that arched up like the jagged back of a green dragon. I thought about the university I was leaving behind. How was it that I had gotten into one of America's best schools? Me, from Chicago, from the west side of that vast and consumptive city. Working-class, ethnic, all the high-spirited sins America proudly touts.

In the fifties and sixties when I was growing up, Chicago was a quilt of neighborhoods—Poles and Irish and Italians, Russians and Germans and Bohemians. Not the beatnik bohemians. These were the people who came from Bohemia deep inside what is now the Czech Republic. People flowed into Chicago like a turbid gushing river. Everyone in search of a job in the mills, the factories, the slaughterhouses. We too, the Moreau family, were immigrants. But for us it was from Montreal. Yet, we melted with everyone else in that great post-war stewpot.

Walking down the neighborhood streets on any nice spring or summer day, step by step as you went along, rich smells from the kitchens drifted from the open windows. Dark Russian black bread, Italian sausage heavily laced with fennel, Bohemian roast duck.

I had done well in college, pushing the immigrant work ethic to its limit, then applied to a few graduate schools, of which Johns Hopkins was one. Doing so almost out of sheer amusement. The letter arrived. I was in. I remember reading it thinking there must be a mistake. They accidentally left off the words: 'We regret to inform you....' But they hadn't. It was real.

I looked out the window of the Pinto and watched the sultry green hills spin past us. A certain sense of guilt, a certain sense of personal betrayal, crept through me. The look on the face of Dr. Markham. I could see it perfectly. A look that said—and meant—'Goodbye, Alex.'

We screamed through Virginia. Soon we were deep into the countryside of the Carolinas. Little Pinto performed flawlessly as she snapped up the miles. Stef drove and we talked. The radio crackled from station to station, each one offering many versions of country music. Warm air gushed in through the window.

I thought about how I had met Stef shortly after I'd arrived in Baltimore. Walking across campus, I noticed a character stretched out flat on his back on the quadrangle grass holding a camera with a two-thousand-millimeter lens, staring intently up into a tree, now and then pulling the camera to his eye and snapping a picture. I watched for a moment and then walked over. Stef sat up, cross-legged, and explained that he was photographing a finch in the tree. I looked up to see a beautiful yellow and black bird.

Stefan Kale was as Baltimore as the Orioles—born and raised there. He was the son of Joshua Kale, a fire-and-brimstone Baptist minister who as a young preacher had come bounding into the big city from a small town in West Virginia, entrusted with a poor parish in a working-class neighborhood of East Baltimore known as Highlandtown. There, Joshua and his wife Sara raised a big family of eight children—four sons and four daughters, Stef being the youngest of the lot.

They lived in the tight quarters of a Baltimore row house next to the church of Joshua Kale's ministry—ten people squeezed into six rooms. Joshua was a breathtakingly handsome man with light brown hair and crystalline blue emotive eyes. A good jaw that tolerated a smile well when given the chance. He'd dress in preacher black, and as he walked the streets of Highlandtown you could spot him from a block away. Bible in hand, steady gait. As he passed row houses stacked side to side like dominos, people would say, "Mornin' there, Revern'." He'd answer with a slight nod and a touch of a smile. "Mornin'."

Then one bright Sunday in April when Stef was twelve, as Joshua Kale bellowed his Sunday sermon, pacing across the front of the church, suddenly the young preacher ceased talking. He stared cold and empty at his congregation and hunched over and clutched his chest. His face paled and he fell dead right there in front of his flock.

Young Stef, who each and every Sunday had been dragged to church and forced to glut upon Joshua's chilling words of sin and punishment sat in the back of the choir loft with his hand up the blouse of Jennifer O'Malley, a busty mature thirteen year old who giggled and squirmed as Stef deftly unclasped the hook of her bra.

"I'm sure the lightning bolt that struck old Josh was really meant for me," Stef often confessed. "I'm sure it was a case of mistaken identity. Poor Josh. Just damn lousy aim, I suppose."

With the family untied by Joshua's death, Stef took to the streets. He hung out in the coffee houses on Calvert Street and snuck into the jazz clubs through the back door. He met an artist, a painter named Thomas Jefferson Smith, ten years Stef's senior. Jefferson, as he was called, was a tall black man who shaved his head and wore a beret and had a neat little goatee. Together, the two roamed the old streets of Baltimore. It was during those days that Stef learned to use a camera. Jefferson had a Leica that he had acquired as payment for a painting. But being the abstract painter he was, the camera, with all its unnecessary precision and gadgetry, annoyed Jefferson beyond all rational reason.

"Here, Stef, take this thing, will you? Do what you want with it. I don't care—hock it, or don't do anything. Just take it."

Soon, that camera became an extension of Stef's being—the hardware of his soul. Wherever he went, whatever he did, it was Stef and Jefferson and the Leica.

CHAPTER FOUR

The green hills of North Carolina were all around us. Dark hills that shaded the setting sun. Stef pushed the speed limit. A sheltering sky leaned across the rolling mountains, cutting through smoky clouds, tracing the tops of the hills like delicate lace. I watched the hills sink into darkness as we raced past them. I wondered about life in those mountains. Once there was a time when I thought it would be terrible to be trapped in a place such as this. Now, a bit older, all life seemed correct. None was right and none was wrong, and more and more I found myself looking with envy at a simple life. The green hills were alive. They seemed to breathe and I had the feeling they were watching us. I wondered what they thought as we rumbled through their backyard in such a great hurry.

I pulled a writing tablet and a pen from my pack in the back seat. At the top of the page I wrote, *June 5, 1980,* and set down these words that I would send to my parents:

Dear Mom and Dad,
I am now two hundred miles south of Baltimore heading

*south in a green Ford Pinto with Stefan Kale. It's diffi-
cult for me to say this, but I quit science. I just couldn't
continue any longer. I know you were as excited as I
once was about my fellowship at MIT, but I was drained
just thinking about it. I let them know I will not be coming to the lab. I'm sure it will be hard for you to hear
this. It was hard for me do it, but I had to. I don't know
where we are going exactly. Mexico and other places.
I'm not sure where. All will be fine. I will be out of touch
by phone for quite a while I suspect, but will try to get
off a card or a letter whenever I can.
I love you both. I'll be thinking of you and the gang.
Take care and don't worry, and get to a Cubbies game
for me!
Alex.*

I slipped the letter into an envelope and wrote the address on the front and stuck a stamp on it, and listened to the quiet hum of the tires on the pavement below us.

It was nearly dark; the air had cooled. The thrashing of cars on the interstate had let up as the road opened. We talked about a multitude of things. Stef talked about his many years on the road.

"We'd be in Texas by morning, if we could drive all night, that is," Stef pronounced. "I could do it easily…drive all day and all night. One time I drove for three days nonstop at full speed. And once I drove from Baltimore to New Orleans and back, non-stop. Twenty hours to New Orleans, twenty minutes there, and twenty hours back again."

Stef's wanderlust flowed up from a place deep in his soul, unleashed and untied by the death of Josh. He would work for months at any job he could find and then load his backpack—always light and always with camera—and take to the road. If he had no car, his thumb or the rails were more than suitable. He could always count on the rails, but he dreaded the yard bulls that stalked the boxcars in search of hobos. The bulls could be mean to the point of vicious, knowing that most of the time they were dealing with humanity that barely clung to the lowest rung of the ladder.

I looked at my watch. "We should stop and eat." The radio twanged as we tore across South Carolina.

"Florence, two miles," Stef announced. "Sounds like a place you'd want to eat."

A cluster of lights lit the road up ahead. We turned off the interstate onto a street that circled into downtown Florence—a small pretty place, southern and drowsy—predictable as a nickel.

"I'm thinking Florence is dry," I said, as we crept through town. "Not a saloon anywhere yet."

Some things about Florence were obvious right away. It was conservative. It had that feeling about it. And religious, churches abounding. And of course, southern—very, very southern. That seemed to be Florence: churches, country folk, and Spanish moss dripping like cobwebs from the trees and telephone lines.

We drove twice up and down Main Street. Hardly anything was open, just an all-night convenience store and a gas station. It was hard to believe that even in a small town like Florence not a single restaurant would be open at eight o'clock in the evening. I began to think that life in a rural town wasn't for me after all. With no other choice, we headed back toward the interstate when at last I saw it.

"Look, Stef! A place!" I shouted.

Stef swung the car wide and headed back to what appeared to be a restaurant. A neon sign glowed in the window. We got out of the car and stretched legs that had become locked in rigor, and went inside. The restaurant was small and embarrassingly simple. We sat at a table. Soon, a young pretty waitress came over. She had lush brown hair that hung loose. Deep green eyes.

"How y'all doing?" she asked.

"Fine." I looked at the menu.

"Could we get a couple of beers?" Stef asked.

"Sure can." She came back with two beers and two glasses. "Y'all travelin'?" she asked. "Where ya headin'?"

"South," I said.

"Ain't this the South?"

"Well, yeah, but we're going far south," Stef said.

"Oh, you mean like Flor-da or something."

"Something like that," I said. "Actually we're going to Central America."

"Central 'merica! Whew! That is far south. What you going there for? I don't think I'd like it there. People are crazy there. They speak English down there? No, not me," she said. "I don't even like going to Flor-da. I like it right here. Y'all want to order now?"

"We'll have a pizza," Stef said. "What kind do you have?"

"Reg-lar pizza," she said.

"Okay, then we'll have a reg-lar pizza," I said. "And make it big, we're real hungry."

She smiled and winked, and off to the kitchen. When she brought our pizza, she sat at the table and talked while we ate. She got a beer and pulled off a slice of pizza for herself.

"What's your name?" Stef asked.

"Elvira," she said, looking around the room coyly with big green eyes. She wore a cotton top thin as tissue paper that clung to her body and tight across her breasts. It was clear she knew how this looked and how to use it with great skill as she leaned snuggly back in the chair and took deep breaths, then leaned over the table so that the impression of her taut nipples pressed firmly against her blouse.

"Someday, maybe I'll go far away, too," Elvira said, daintily. She liked to look at Stef, reaching out with her cool eyes. "I get real lonely sometimes. Just working here and livin' in Florence."

"You need a friend," I said.

"A what?"

"You need a friend, a lover."

"I got one of them. I got a man if that's what you mean." Elvira blew hair out of her eye and shot some icy green in my direction. "I sure don't need *another*, that's for sure."

"Are you married?" Stef said.

"Nope."

"Then it's easy. Get a new lover."

"It ain't so easy in Florence, South Care-lina," Elvira said. "The men's all the same down here. They love that bottle more'n they love their women. Spendin' all their nights with a whiskey bottle." She turned momentarily away and poked out her lip.

"What I really need is a different kind of man. Even a Yankee. I know a girl that's got herself a Yankee and they's real happy...y'all are Yankees, ain't you?"

Stef sort of nodded. "I guess you could say. So where's your boyfriend now?"

"Hell, I don't know," Elvira said. "He don't tell me where he goes. Ain't none of my business, that's what he says." Elvira sipped her beer. I saw her glance quickly at Stef. "I suppose y'all be headin' outta here tonight."

I looked at my watch. It was nine fifteen. "Can't go," I said. "We're not allowed to drive after ten o'clock." I explained the situation with the car.

Elvira's eyes glowed.

"Is there a motel around?" I asked.

"Not in Florence. Not close by, anyway. Just local folk here," Elvira said. "Don't need no motels."

"That's too bad," Stef replied. "We need a place to sleep."

Just then someone came to the door of the restaurant. Elvira jumped from her chair and intercepted him and backed him onto the porch. I could hear traces of a conversation but couldn't see the man, hidden in the dim porch light. Elvira kept him far back.

Stef took a hard slug of beer. "Whew, mate, we have a hot one here. Whew! I think we've found some real southern comfort. Did you see her? Boy, I could barely eat my pizza."

"Well, I don't know. Stef, I don't think it's all that easy...besides, there's what's-his-name lurking about."

Elvira came back and sat at the table. She tried to talk as

though nothing had happened, but she was jittery and uncomfortable. She got up, cleared the table and asked if we wanted anything more. Another beer, maybe? When she returned with the beer, she seemed to have undergone a miraculous recovery of spirit. She started toying with Stef, even rubbing her hands through his hair. The room seemed to be getting hotter by the minute. I could only imagine what would happen next. I pictured Elvira taking off her clothes right there in the restaurant, flinging this piece that way, that piece this way, and when the last stitch of clothing had spun across the room, what's-his-name would bolt through the front door, drunk and mean and waving a gun—hurling useless warnings to us all before sending us to Boot Hill somewhere outside Florence. That never happened, though it might have, and there were moments when I was sure Elvira's cotton top couldn't last much longer.

From the kitchen, someone yelled, "We're closing folks. Time to go. Wrap it up Elvie."

"That's TJ," Elvira explained. "He wants to go home." Elvira took away the empty beer bottles as we got up to leave.

"Y'all don't have to go now," Elvira said.

"That's not what TJ thinks," Stef said.

"TJ don't tell me nothing," Elvira flared.

"Well, we've got to find a place to sleep," I said. I looked around impatiently.

Stef said, "We'll sleep in the car. We'll find a place along the road and pull over and sleep in the car. That's all we can do."

"That's a good ide-er," Elvira raved. "Y'all can park out back. They's plenty of room out there and I live right upstairs."

Ho-ly shit! My mind was a blur and all I wanted to do was stretch out and close my eyes and fall into a deep sleep. Elvira went back into the kitchen. Stef and I huddled to discuss this.

"This is it, Alex. I can't stop now," he begged.

I had to agree. I was too tired not to. "All right," I said. "We'll park out back and I'll crash and you can wait for Elvira."

Stef drove behind the restaurant to a big open lot where there were a couple of junked cars. There was a house off to the left and another one behind the lot. Stef got out and headed to the restaurant. I climbed into the back seat and made a pillow out of a jacket. I looked up at the house where Elvira lived. Lights were on and the window was open. A breeze pulled the curtains out into the night. I felt calm and good and very tired. The air was cool and delicious. As if drugged, I faded off into a calm easy sleep.

CHAPTER FIVE

June 6, 1980 – Day 5

By nine o'clock the next morning, we were a hundred miles from Florence. Little Pinto ripped up mile after mile. In Atlanta we stopped for coffee and breakfast. After eating, we stood in the parking lot of the truck stop in the clear morning air chewing toothpicks the way the truckers do. We climbed into the car. I took to the wheel, driving out onto the interstate in the sweet morning sun. I felt as good as I ever have at any point in my life. I was full of energy and ambition and talk. Stef sat next to me slugging coffee. He looked terrible. Ain't life grand!

We hoped to make it to Texas by nightfall and, except to gas-up and use the can, we drove nonstop. Out of Georgia and into the sleek Alabama countryside, passing one small town after another. An endless stream of threadbare shacks and plots of thinly planted crops and rickety old school buses that belched plumes of thick black powder high into the sky.

When we pulled through the small towns of Alabama, people looked at us as if we were part of a strange parade, some even waved. Going through Alabama made me feel sad in a way that even a perfect morning couldn't improve.

We arrived in Mississippi, pushing little Pinto hard, going seventy and seventy-five and even eighty miles an hour, never seeing a patrol car in all of Alabama or Mississippi. Too hot, perhaps, for the police.

The sky was without a cloud and the sun beat down all afternoon. At midday we passed through the town of Meridian. The air, what there was of it, was thick as blackstrap molasses—my skin dripped moisture from every pore. I felt like one of those jumbo gulf shrimp being slow-boiled out in the afternoon sun. I no longer looked at the countryside around us because wherever I looked, I saw only heat and the blanched and parched wood of the houses and buildings—the slow eyes of the people. When I lived in Chicago, I wondered what drove the original settlers to live in a climate of long endless winters. Now, I wondered the same about Mississippi, with its festering heat.

We passed through Jackson. Stef rose up from the back seat.

"You can sleep back there?" I asked. "In all this heat?"

"How long was I out?" he asked.

"Couple of hours...maybe more."

"I feel better." He climbed into the front seat.

I told him we were in Mississippi. He said we'd make it to Fort Worth by evening and smiled the first good smile I'd seen all day. Then he reached over and rapped me on the shoulder and started singing songs about traveling. Songs like "Ventura Highway" and "Mexico." A song I knew well came on the radio: Fleetwood Mac's Stevie Nicks singing "Landslide." I turned the volume up loud. Now the words seemed truer than ever. My eyes misted over as the words fell from my lips:

Well I've been 'fraid of changin'...

Stef leaned back and caught the rush of air through the window. "Mate," he said, "I feel damn good." I looked over, and seeing him happy and rested made me feel good too. I looked again at the countryside and I began to like Mississippi a little more.

We slid into Louisiana by climbing a gigantic bridge that arched high over the Mississippi River. There it was. The aorta of America. A great girth of swirling currents. A tough river filled with heavy air and rich fragrances. Barges churned up and down as river mist clung in patches above the water, as horns from the boats groaned long and low. We sped down the toe of the bridge. I planted the gas pedal onto the floor, taking little Pinto up to ninety or more.

Through Shreveport, Louisiana, and then into Texas. Pinto devoured the miles like a road junkie. When we crossed into Texas, she broke into a high gallop. We drove through eastern Texas, but I remember none of it until out before us was a mass of flickering lights—Dallas and Fort Worth.

CHAPTER SIX

June 6, 1980 – Day 5

S ome things in this world never change. They never get better and they never get worse—they are immutable. Here forever. Used car lots are one of those things. They are the same today as yesterday, tomorrow as today—the cockroaches of man's creativity.

Cortina Motors was a typical place. Cars in neat little rows with big white numbers painted on the windshields: $1,595 or $995 or no price at all, just the word *SALE!*

Behind the lot was a sad little shack, the office. A string of lights trimmed the lot. Strips of cheap plastic flags were laced from the office out over the cars—cars with all the looks of questionable origin. It was 9 p.m. One by one, rows of lights were shut off. Cortina Motors was being put to bed.

We pulled into a dusty lot. Instantly, a man lurched from the office and jostled up to our car, briskly, as though we were the first customers of the day.

"Ozzie's the name," he piped. He stuck out a big Texas hand for us to shake, and he put on a big Texas smile full of raw gums and large teeth. His forehead shined ever as much as the gleam of his hair. We stated our business. "We're delivering this Pinto," Stef said, tapping her fondly on the dash. We climbed out of the car and followed Ozzie to the office—a mournful looking place inside and out.

"Esther, these folks is delivern' that Ford Pinto out there," Ozzie said to a woman sitting behind an old metal desk.

Esther—fiftyish, honest and sincere looking, Baptist no doubt—rummaged through a stack of papers. I asked Ozzie why the Pinto was being returned to Texas.

"Being re-po-sessed," he said.

All at once, I felt betrayed, tricked. Like some strong-armed loan shark who was twisting the fingers of a distressed victim. Even if the owner wasn't making payments on the Pinto, I was sad to be partaking in Ozzie's deal.

"Get these nice fellers a hunner dollars," Ozzie told Esther. She opened a cash box, took out a stack of bills, and pecked off five twenty-dollar notes. She turned them over and did it again, snapping each of them one at a time. Same total. She handed the money to me. I shoved it snuggly into my pocket. It was late and all I wanted was to get out of Fort Worth.

"We're going to the border," Stef said to Ozzie. "Is there a bus station in town?"

"On the west side," Ozzie replied. He turned to Esther. "How's about you give these nice fellers a lift to the Greyhound on your way home?"

Esther obliged.

When everything was done, when Cortina Motors was closed up snug and tight, we climbed into the front of Esther's massive

Buick Electra—a big eight-mile-to-the-gallon affair.

Esther turned the key and started the car. The dashboard lit up like a carnival ride in blistering green and red and white lights. She punched the pedal to the floor and we took off through the downtown streets of Fort Worth at a petrifying pace, through street lights turned yellow (and a red one), wheeling the car wide around corners. Through it all Esther talked in some slow Texas accent I couldn't make head or tail of. Soon (very soon!) we arrived at the bus depot, and once there, right in front of it and not a second sooner, Esther planted her foot on the brake, terminating the momentum of that gargantuan craft, throwing Stef and me to the dashboard.

"Well, boys, here yus are," Esther said politely and proudly. "Y'all be careful now and enjoy yer travelin'. If yer ever in these parts agin, be sure to stop in and see us, won't ya?"

We thanked Esther, grabbed our packs, and on wobbly legs went into the bus depot. We were two days from Baltimore, four hundred miles from the Mexican border, tired and anxious. We bought two tickets to Laredo that cost forty dollars each. Damn painful to spend nearly ten percent of what I had just to go through Texas. We paid the fare and climbed onto a big, mostly empty, scenicruiser. By midnight the bus was barreling down Highway 35 toward Old Mexico.

I was up early the next morning. A silver Texas sun splashed down on the same sad piece of earth it had blasted the day before. I watched empty Texas. Little by little I felt the hard white land that flowed next to us pull me away from my past. I was reinforced in my decision to leave Baltimore, in my choice to rescind a life I had once so auspiciously and diligently selected and nurtured.

I recovered from my wallet the sheet of paper on which I had written Thoreau's words and, like a monk reading the daily office, I quietly read, "...*and not, when I came to die, discover that I had not lived.*" I folded the paper and replaced it with great care in my wallet.

Stef slept on until we arrived at Laredo. We got out, went to the border, and walked across a little bridge that humped over the Rio Grande.

"There she is," Stef beamed, "The Big River." We looked down on the strip of water—this one, an anemic trickle of ooze and effluence with all the truculent vapors that went with it. The saddest part of civilization now as a barrier between two burly countries. An irreverent message to the traveler—sighted or blind—marking passage between two nations.

On the Mexican side, we got our visas stamped and went to the first bar we came to, a dusty lonely border bar called Del Gato. We walked into a room filled with the smells of Mexico—tortillas and pollo con mole and goat cheese. I was happy and busting with excitement, having quickly banished my soul of the bad Texas blues.

I looked around the shadowy bar at the scattering of people: Mexicans and the occasional Americans who cross the border for the good cheap beer. A radio played songs of mariachis. I felt wonderful. The bartender came over and stood in front of us, waiting patiently.

"Dos cervezas," I said.

The beer arrived and we ordered shots of tequila. I took the tequila, smelled its musty odor, its harsh fragrance, drank it, then drowned it with a slug of beer. Stef watched and laughed and did the same and slammed the shot glass down onto the counter. It was a hell of a breakfast.

CHAPTER SEVEN

June 7, 1980 – Day 6

After breakfast, we gathered our things and headed across Nuevo Laredo to the bus depot. What a place! Dirty, crowded, confusing. Buses going everywhere. Stef took a map from his pack and spread it out. We would go far into Mexico right away, that was our plan, as far as the city of San Luis Potosi. We bought a ticket that cost a hundred and thirty pesos, about six dollars, compared to the forty-odd dollars we'd spent to go half that distance in Texas.

Once again we were moving—curling down a narrow highway that nips the bleak desert of northern Mexico. The land was bare. The air was dusty and hot. The bus rumbled through the hard hot desert. I leaned back in the seat and watched as raw parched land skidded past us. Empty land, bad as could be—poor and sad and soulful. Land to live on but not to live off of. We scrolled past poor Mexican families scattered about in lonely huts living on a hot hellish Earth.

I stared out the window and watched the whispering sands of vanishing Mexico. With each mile we covered, I felt my past fall imperceptibly away like the dust that sprayed up behind the bus and blended invisibly into the air.

Next to me was an old man with the sweetest face I had ever seen. He sat peacefully minding his business. Eventually, the boredom of the hollow desert and a certain curiosity about us must have gotten to him. He leaned over and politely he asked, "Where are you two going?" I told him and then he started talking. He was a Mexican named Jose Ramirez, born in 1889. He took out an American driver's license and, indeed, there in the space marked date-of-birth were the numbers 4-14-89: Jose Ramirez was ninety-one years old. Then he told me of his life.

"I fought in the Mexican Revolution of 1915-16, first fighting for the Mexican army until I got shot in the leg. Then I thought, maybe I'm fighting for the wrong side. So I turned and fought with the guerrillas."

He pulled up his pant leg and showed where the bullet had torn through his calf.

"In 1920 I fled to the States. I went to Chicago, where I got a job and never missed a day of work, even during the depression—not one day. I would do any work there was, all the jobs no else wanted to do." Jose said this with the pride of a man who had struggled and won, someone who could sit tall and straight even as an old man. Someone who could say 'I took the worst there was, and I did my best.'

For twenty years, Jose hadn't been able to return to Mexico because he'd had no papers. But now he was a US citizen and twice a year he took the bus from Chicago to the desert town of Queretaro in central Mexico where his brother, who was ninety-three, lived. We talked for hours. Everything Jose said I believed because it made such good sense that even if it wasn't true, it should have been. Then I told Jose I grew up on the west side of Chicago.

This brought great delight to him. He chuckled full and deep, and when he did, his wrinkled face smoothed out and his brown eyes danced and he slapped himself on the leg. Some old lost memories of the west side of Chicago had been resurrected and he couldn't wait to tell me of them.

"Oh, ha, ha, ha," Jose laughed so hard. "Oh, ha, ha...that's where Al Capone lived, you know."

"I know," I replied. "But long before my time, of course."

But not before Jose's time. "I worked in speakeasies, too," he said. "You see, they liked to hire us because we kept our mouths shut. We were wetbacks, you know. Well, first I shined shoes, then I tended bar. I didn't mind. It was good money and I saved every penny of it and bought a two-flat on West Diversey Street. I lived there over fifty years. Raised a family there. My youngest son is a doctor," he said, brimming with pride.

On and on Jose went. He talked and I listened. The bus blasted down the two-lane highway, passing cars at eighty miles an hour, swinging out into the lane of oncoming traffic or off to the right onto the crumbly shoulder. At each town, we pulled up to a small depot near the plaza. With engine purring, people got off and people got on and loads of merchandise were exchanged and people waved from the windows of the bus or from the depot and again we were off.

The villages were simple and sleepy. When we pulled into one of these humble-down places, a new bus driver came on and the old one disappeared. Then later, far down the road, the first driver was back at the wheel and the second driver vanished. All day it went like that as the drivers took turns guiding us through the sparse desert. I watched and wondered where the driver went when he wasn't driving. In fact, there was nowhere for him to go— nowhere for anyone to go. All the seats were filled. *How can you hide on a bus*, I thought? Yet one driver drove, and one driver disappeared.

Finally, when we stopped at a village, I said, "Jose, what happens to the driver who's not driving? He disappears. I never see him on the bus."

Jose pulled me over to the window and pointed below.

"*No!*" I said, "That's the baggage compartment!" I watched and sure enough, just before the bus left, when the luggage was stored and the bus was loaded and the people had boarded, one of the drivers climbed into the baggage compartment. The other driver shut the door and locked it.

"There's no room for him in the bus," Jose said. "The company would never permit that."

"You mean he rides down there locked inside like a suitcase?"

"Si"

I slumped back into my seat.

The bus roared on through the desert for two, maybe three, hours. Again we stopped. I bought two mangos from a boy at the depot, tossed one to Stef through the open bus window, and looked into the compartment where the extra driver rode. There it was— an ugly empty baggage bay with a dirty sheet across the bare floor.

No room to sit up, no lights. On the wall a crucifix hung—not a cabin but a coffin. As before, one of the drivers climbed inside and the door was closed and locked. I boarded the bus and took my seat. I looked sadly at Jose.

"Men need to work," he said. "That's how it is down here."

Surely no one understood this better than Jose.

We passed through the cities of Monterrey and Saltillo, two industrial cities in the north of Mexico. Foundries and factories and mills with dirty smokestacks and huge open industrial drains that puked waste into the local water supply. The men in these cities reminded me of coal miners. Pulling through in the afternoon as the factories were letting out, the street corners were clogged with sooty-faced men, heads wrapped in bandanas and bodies thick with muscle like racehorses. They waited for a bus to take them to their shacks on the edge of town, to dinners of beans and tortillas and tequila. It was clear that cities like this are the spine of Mexico, and what a tough spine it is.

There was an ugly charm to these places, but there was no beauty. When we left, it felt good to be leaving. We rode for an hour or more. I became sleepy and the countryside became monotonous. The desert was more bare than ever, only an occasional adobe hut—always with a wisp of smoke that rose to the sky like a cobra. Land that was raw and thirsty and bare. Tumbleweed tumbled across the desert, caught in a tailspin of wind. My mouth was dry. I tried to suck saliva to keep it wet. I wondered how hot it must be down in the baggage bay, big wheels spitting heat onto the tin belly of the bus.

We passed the town of Matehuala three hundred miles below

the border. Poverty, that persistent affliction of Mexico, was still there, but it was poverty of a different kind. There is a difference between being poor and being destitute, between being penniless and being impoverished. These people were poor and penniless, but they were not destitute. I sensed none of the desperation the border festers.

The bus stopped at a roadside restaurant and the driver held up his hand. "Viente minutos," he called out. People filed off the bus into the restaurant. Only old Jose Ramirez stayed on the bus. From a sack he kept below his feet he took out a sandwich and fruit and spread these on his lap. I promised Jose we'd be back shortly. We went and had lunch of enchiladas verde with beans and rice and a stack of tortillas.

"I feel great, Alex," Stef said. "There's so much to see. So much to photograph. Just look at this. I'm telling you, I'm going nuts. I can't believe it. And tomorrow we'll be in...where will we be?" Stef asked, as he packed beans and tortillas into his mouth.

"San Luis Potosi," I said. "We'll be there tonight."

We ate our lunch and drank a bottle of beer and together everything cost barely a dollar each. Now we were living!

We boarded the bus and for the first time I realized Stef and I were the only Gringos there. Suddenly we were different. As we walked down the aisle, children with big pumpkin eyes leaned from their seats and stared at Stef's blond hair and blue eyes and blond beard. The young ones, the niños, had never seen anyone like him—only those statues and paintings in church of that man who looked like Stef. And now here he was riding on their bus.

Late that night, we pulled into the bus station in San Luis

Potosi. We said goodbye to Jose, who wished us luck and told us to watch out for the guerillas, an oddly true statement now more than sixty years since Jose's encounter. From the station, we watched Jose's happy smiling face. He sat next to the window and waved as the bus headed into the night. I was going to miss Jose and his good stories and peaceful eyes.

The bus station in San Luis was new and big and modern, and out on the edge of town. We walked into the still night air toward the lights of town. On down the road slowly—nowhere to go, nowhere to be—and then up ahead I saw a simple small motel along the highway. But all we really needed was a patch of clean grass where we could pitch our tent. I asked the desk clerk if we could put our tent up out back.

He gave a nod and said, "Si, senior. Viente pesos."

We paid the money and went behind the motel. I stretched out on the soft grass and looked up at the sky. Now, for the first time in three days, my body was free of cramped rigid seats. I lay blissfully in one flat uninterrupted plane and watched the universe shimmer high above. We talked and listened to the desert, to its pure silence. I watched the sky, vast and full and flickering. I could see the entire universe—every holy piece of it. Soon I fell into a deep and blessed sleep.

CHAPTER EIGHT

June 8, 1980 – Day 7

The next day was Sunday. All morning church bells rang out from the steeples of the cathedrals and churches of San Luis. The whole city made its way to Mass. In the afternoon, lovers strolled blithely down the narrow cobbled streets. Old men played checkers in the parks.

We went to the mercado. Stef photographed for a while. We ate lunch at one of the cheap market stalls and drank Corona. Lunch cost fifty cents. It was a wonderful market—a grand kaleidoscope of color and motion and activity, things to smell and things to touch and things to eat. Our senses were drenched. As we walked along, Stef said, "For dinner we'll make a big pot of vegetable stew."

We bought everything we needed: a large cabbage, potatoes, onions, carrots, squash, salt and pepper, and four birotes—small loaves of fresh Mexican bread. The birotes were right out of the oven and still warm. We couldn't resist eating one as we ambled through the market. And we bought a pineapple so big and ripe it oozed juice from a crack in the bottom. Damn, what a meal it would be!

We walked back to our camp on the edge of town. The afternoon temperature rocketed to a hundred and onward. The motel where we were staying had a pool, and since we were honorable paying guests, of sorts, it seemed only right that we should make use of it. Thus we did.

Sitting alongside the pool, we watched two of the most beautiful women I'd ever seen. Gorgeous Mexican women in their early twenties. They had perfect black hair and cinnamon skin and sleek bodies, and they wore tiny bikinis—barely anything at all. They were staying at the motel also, traveling I suppose, and each was guarded by a suspicious husband who didn't like the looks of the two Gringo voyeurs spying their women.

We spent the entire afternoon sitting by the water, watching the women as they made love to us from the other side, bending and turning and jumping and bouncing and winking and running delicate fingers through their hair. As they did this, their men strutted—chests puffed out and stomachs sucked in, trying like jealous pigeons to recover the attention of their women.

"Jesus! Have you ever seen such beautiful women!" Stef said. The women carried on mercilessly. When we went into the water, they went into the water—diving, then standing and rearranging their suits to make sure all was in place and everything was properly covered, though at times it wasn't, as much to their delight as ours. They swam through the water with broad mermaid-like strokes or smooth breaststrokes, then got out and walked daringly around the pool.

About six o'clock, when the sun was winding down and dinner time neared, we took our things and went back to our tent.

The next day, Stef went out to photograph the old city. I found a small café and wrote a postcard to Maureen.

Dear, Dear, Dear Maureen,

Am now in the town of San Luis Potosi in central Mexico. Made record-breaking time getting to the border and then down here on a Mexican bus. So far at least the buses are not too bad. Clean, for the most part. I hope everything is going along fine up in Baltimore. I know I shouldn't belabor the point, but leaving science was the right thing to do. Every day I feel more certain of it. For the first time in years, I feel as though I can think, really think, without being pushed this way or that. Everything I do seems different now, even in the span of one short week. My eyes and ears have been opened and I think it's only going to get better.

The only downside is that I miss you this much (I am holding my arms apart as far as they go)! If you hate me, I'll understand. Maybe I didn't handle things very well there at the end. I wasn't thinking so clearly, I guess. Still, I know this is the right thing to do.

Can't squeeze any more on this card so I'll have to end now. Next stop, a place called San Miguel de Allende.

Yes, I do love you.

Alex (aka Alejandro...ha, ha).

p.s. If you get a call from my parents, be sure to tell them I'm fine.

We stayed in San Luis for two days, doing little but drinking beer and watching the Mexican women at the pool in the beastly hot afternoon. But by the third day, we were itching to leave. On the map, the village of San Miguel de Allende was halfway between San Luis Potosi and Mexico City. Life there would be wonderful—cafés and restaurants and the artists from all over the world who flee to the desert town to hide out and work. We bought bus tickets and once again took off through the desert, farther south, farther south.

The desert below San Luis is bare, open, hopeless land that grows nothing but rocks and dust, and to be out in it in the daytime is dangerous even for a short while. It is not at all kind to life. The land is flat for as far as you can see, except for a ridge of mountains far, far off in the distance. We never seemed to get to those mountains no matter how long we traveled—I considered that they were only a mirage, a dirty trick my eyes played on my brain. Stef sat next to the window. A current of warm air came rushing in. It was good air so long as we were in the bus and not out in the desert trapped in the heat.

We talked. Stef looked out the window as he spoke, always watching, always seeing, always waiting for the one moment when he would pull the camera to his eye, focus, and release four or five frames. I thought photographs taken like that would be hopeless. But that was because I had no talent as a photographer, and Stef was a genius with the camera. I rarely had enough talent even to see a good image and no ability to capture it on film. I would say, "Stef, quick, look!" and point to something as it whizzed past the bus and evaporated behind us in a cloud of desert powder. It was no use. My eyes lived in the present; that was not soon enough. Stef's eyes saw things that hadn't yet happened—things that were about to happen. He saw the future and stored it for us to look back on.

As we sat on the bus rolling toward San Miguel de Allende, I again sensed the surge of life that had been missing while buried under the tonnage of graduate work. I had nothing to do but what I wanted to do. I was again a child, and with that freedom I found a child's enthusiasm and delight in the world around me and in the discovery of that world. When I looked out the window, I saw what was there, not what was inside my mind. When I smelled something, it smelled fresh and clean, or putrid and rotten. I thought about those smells and found a trueness and honesty in everything—everything had meaning. Everything on this planet had purpose and I, too, had a new purpose and was wonderfully curious about every fractured inch of life around me. When I saw a child, I thought about children. I realized what it meant when they say we are only as strong as the weakest among us. And when I saw Stef, I saw a person I'd never known, though I'd known him for years. I was discovering everything. I was out of my little world of science and theories and experiments. I had uncoupled my mind from the old train to which it had been tethered. Now the engine was free to roam. I was the engineer who would let that happen.

CHAPTER NINE

June 11, 1980 – Day 10

We arrived in San Miguel late in the afternoon. From the bus station, we walked down a twisted street to the zocalo in the heart of town where we were surrounded by marvelous weather-worn buildings with balconies trimmed in fine wrought iron. Across from us was a proud old cathedral. Pigeons perched in coveys on the high ledges below the glittering stained-glass windows. Out beyond the city, magic mountains loomed.

The zocalo was awash in the lost light of late afternoon as the sun set behind the city. We would get a room for the night—a hotel room with a real bed and clean sheets and a pillow and a bath. *What a thought!*

Big opulent hotels faced the zocalo. I went and inquired about the prices and picked a nice one, a place called La Hotel Cabrillo. A stately old residence with a lobby made of granite and marble and Mexican tiles and melancholy ceiling fans that turned slowly high above. Yes, this is where we would stay.

Looking around the lobby, I saw fancy waiters rush from the kitchen, trays banked high overhead, drinks and wine and cold beer for patrons and guests in the lobby. Hungry smells of all kinds leaked from the kitchen. We checked into a room, a simple but grand place, and yet all I wanted was a long cool bath.

That evening we ate dinner at a café near the zocalo. Enchiladas with mole, beans and rice, a stack of tortillas. Beer to drink and a cup of dark coffee to finish. We watched the zocalo bustle with activity. About eight o'clock people began to collect in the square. A mariachi band with guitars and trumpets and a big bass fiddle set up in the gazebo in the center of the zocalo.

"Will you look at that," Stef said. "It's a festival."

People came down the winding streets that ended in the zocalo. Everyone was happy. Children danced and jumped and ricocheted off each other, and street vendors set up stands selling steamy tacos and cold beer. The air brimmed with grand smells of all kinds. We walked out into the street and suddenly—as if from the sky itself, blasting high from the heavens—the mariachis ripped loose with screaming horns, and all at once the zocalo shook with music. I felt wonderful. We walked into the crowd. Stef watched the señoritas, and the señoritas watched him. They winked and smiled and coaxed him with their hot black eyes and painted lips.

"They're like goddesses," Stef moaned, looking everywhere. "I'm going nuts, Alex, I can't take this." The mariachis wailed and the zocalo rocked and swayed and the music rolled out louder and louder. The saucy eyes of the señoritas got blacker and blacker, and the night seemed to get hotter and hotter.

"I love them all," Stef said. "I'm in love with these women and their gorgeous eyes and that smooth skin and, oh Lord, that hair. I am in love!" Stef let out a good long yelp. The señoritas laughed and taunted him, winking and lifting a shoulder and turning slyly away.

A man inched his way through the crowd toward us. He seemed to be studying us, reading us.

Eventually he said, "Looking for a place to stay? I have a couple of places for rent." His name was Harvey Wetzel, an American from New York City now living in San Miguel. He was lean with thinning gray hair and a desert tan and light blue eyes.

"We have a room for the night," I said. "And after that we'll probably camp outside of town. Anyway, we're not planning to stay for long."

"Well, it's a nice little place, the place I have, just two blocks from here," Harvey Wetzel said, pointing to the road across the square on the other side of the zocalo. "It has a bedroom and a bath and a shower and a living room. And a kitchen with hot and cold water even...the works."

We listened, little interested, as Harvey continued to describe his apartment. Stef said, "How much to rent it?"

"Fifty a month."

"Dollars, you mean?"

"That's right, fifty dollars for a month, or for longer if you want. It's a helluva bargain...a helluva a bargain. Things down here are real cheap, you know. You won't find anything better, that I can tell you for sure. How long have you been here?" Harvey asked.

"We just arrived," I said. "We're traveling, and like I said, we'll be leaving soon. We don't plan to spend a lot of time in one place."

"Well this is the place to be," Harvey said, promptly, unconditionally. "Look at it. What more is there? Why, I've been down here for twenty years probably. I've lived all over the place, every country from here to Panama and I'll tell you what, Miguel is the only place to live." He waited for the music to die down, then said, "I'm from New York. I go back sometimes to visit but, Jesus, I couldn't live there. Nah! Too damn crazy. This place here," he pointed to stone slabs of the zocalo beneath us, "this is where it's at. You guys artists?" he asked, then right away he said, "It's a helluva of a good apartment for fifty bucks. Perfect for an artist."

Music rolled around us as the mariachis blew happy sounds out into the hot Mexican night. Harvey snagged a beer for each of us from one of the vendors. He talked in a nonstop New York kind of prattle. Being in Mexico for twenty years hadn't seemed to have altered that a bit. Some things in life are intractable, I suppose.

It was clear Harvey knew everyone in San Miguel. He talked to the Mexicans in Spanish—New York Spanish. Harvey told us he owned several small homes in San Miguel, although they really belonged to his Mexican wife since only Mexican nationals were permitted to own property. He told us a little about his wife and his marriage; it sounded strangely like a business rather than a marriage. We agreed to meet him the next day to look at the apartment. He told us to enjoy the festival and wandered off into the zocalo.

Stef said, "Christ, Alex, we could stay here for a month real cheap. Fifty bucks for the two of us. Barely a dollar a day each."

It was cheap, all right. "Yeah, San Miguel seems like a good place, but what about traveling, the Yucatan and all that?" I said.

"We don't want to get hung up in one place, do we?"

Stef propositioned that there was still a lot of time for everything, and besides, what was the rush? We were in no hurry. We drank our beer. The mariachis blared. The women were more beautiful than ever. Their black eyes carried us into the night.

CHAPTER TEN

June 12, 1980 – Day 11

When I awoke in the morning I was disoriented and confused and suffering from a nasty hangover. I lay in bed and stared at the high ceiling of the old room, then got up and watched the pretty morning from the French doors that opened onto the street below. I imagined I was in Renaissance Europe. It was 1510, and I was in Rome. Below my window people were talking.

"Michelangelo," a man says, "there is a letter for you from the Holy Father, from the Pope. Come, come quick. Hurry!"

"I have no time now, Antonio. I am busy. I will come later, but I am busy and I am late."

"But Michelangelo, it's from the Pope. He wants to talk to you. It's urgent."

"And I have urgent things to do as well. And when they're finished I will see to the needs of the Pope."

"Shall I tell the messenger that?" Antonio asks. "Shall I tell him that you are too busy for the Holy Father—that Michelangelo has no time for the Pope?"

"If you like. Tell him what you wish, Antonio." They are so inconsiderate when a man is trying to sleep. "You two," I yell, "away...away from my window!"

I got up and washed and returned to the windows and watched the action in the zocalo. It wasn't sixteenth-century Europe. It was twentieth-century Mexico. Cars in the street, pretty women in pastel dresses, beggars, children. All of it below me.

Stef staggered from his bed and shuffled to the bathroom, "I feel like shit," he said.

We went to a café where we ate breakfast and had coffee and watched San Miguel buzz to her morning chores. Stef toted his camera gear. After breakfast he would head out into San Miguel. As we drank coffee, the man at the next table said, "Excuse me, I see you're a photographer."

"That's right," Stef said.

"By God, I haven't seen one of those in years." He pointed to Stef's four-by-five view camera. "It's an old speed graphic, isn't it? Mind if I look?"

Stef handed the camera to the man, who examined it thoughtfully, studying and inspecting it, looking through the viewfinder. He handed the camera back to Stef. "My name's Andy Kozinsky."

"Stefan Kale," Stef replied. "This is my friend, Alex Moreau."

"You must be traveling," Andy said, "because I know everyone in San Miguel who's been here more than a week. Where are you headed?"

"South," I said. "Out to the Yucatan and then to Central

America."

"Yes…the Gringo Trail," Andy said.

"The what?" I asked.

Andy smiled. "It's called the Gringo Trail, what you just described. Once you get to Vera Cruz on the east coast of Mexico, there is just one road to take you down into the Yucatan, along the Caribbean, and into Belize and Guatemala. It's the only road going through that region because the land is either barren or a thick jungle. And it's difficult enough to keep one road open, let alone more than one."

The waitress came by. Andy said, "Pilar, un otro café, por favor. Y una mas para mis amigos tambien. Gracias."

Andy told us more about the Gringo Trail. "You'll meet people coming from the other direction. They'll tell you what's ahead and where to stay and what to watch out for. They'll let you know when the buses are running and what detours to take when the buses are out. People on the Trail rely on each other."

Andy explained about the places to see on the Trail, and the pristine islands off the coast of the Yucatan and Belize, and how to get there. "Time stands still on the Gringo Trail because time is only important for purposes of getting somewhere or keeping an appointment. But once you've arrived at your destination, time is useless. And on the Gringo Trail, there are no destinations…not really."

I asked Andy where he was from and what he was doing in San Miguel.

"Milwaukee, originally," he said. "But that was a long time ago. Since then I've lived in San Francisco, Houston, Virginia,

London, Spain, Portugal, you name it. And now for a few years, here in Miguel."

Andy told us he's a writer. "Miguel understands us, and we understand Miguel," he said. "You see, I'm just one of those hippies from the sixties. I've lived everywhere. I even lived in New York for a while. I thought that's where I had to go to write. But I was dry as that desert out there—and broke no matter how much money I made. Then once while I was in Portugal a friend told me about San Miguel. He said, take two thousand dollars and go there and write a book. I did just that. I spent ten months here and wrote my first novel. There's something about Miguel." Andy looked out to the zocalo. "I don't know what it is," he said pensively, tapping a finger on the rim of his coffee cup, "but it brings out good things in people. It happens over and over here."

He told us about his book. It was called *A Change of Seasons*. I was pretty sure I had heard of it, though I hadn't read it. It did well, Andy explained, and though it didn't make a lot of money, it caught the eyes of the critics. They predicted more good work from him, and that was enough to keep his publisher happy. Now Andy was two-thirds finished with his second book, for which he had been given a substantial advance. He predicted this book would be far better than his first.

"I love it here," Stef told Andy. "I think I could stay here for a long time. We have a chance to rent a place for fifty dollars a month, and I need to do some work, some photography. I'm busting out of my skin because there's so much to photograph here."

Andy placed some coins on the table. "Tonight, come to Las Tortugas," he said. "It's a bar a half a block up on Calle de Cinco de Mayo. We'll all be there."

Stef spent the afternoon photographing the city from up on the hills above San Miguel.

The day was an easy one for me. I wandered through the market and went to look at the house Harvey Wetzel had told us about. It was exactly as he had described. Basic but sufficient. Afterward, I went out to the edge of town where I found a motel named La Siesta. We could camp on the grass behind the motel for a dollar a night, with all the privileges of the hotel.

I walked back to the zocalo and sat at an outside table at the café and ordered a café con leche. I wrote a long letter to Maureen, telling her about our encounters with Harvey Wetzel and Andy Kozinsky and, most of all, about the feeling of relief I had gained from being freed of the grind of graduate school. I told her I liked how the Mexicans lived, and even despite the poverty, how their grip on life seemed more grounded in reality than anything I had ever experienced. I told her again that I missed her. I signed it Alejandro, took it to the post office, and mailed it.

I thought of writing to my parents but decided to wait until morning.

Stef returned, found me sitting at the café, and accused me of being there all day. I told him about all the things I had discovered. He ordered a bottle of Corona and wiped the desert dust from his face—hot and sweaty from the hours in the sun. He told me how, up on the hills, San Miguel was spread out below him like a cluster of jewels on a silky satin desert. White buildings, pastel buildings, cathedrals, a blue sky dotted with clouds, the far-off mountains. How the afternoon sun lit the city in beautiful shades and delicate tones. It was a tough shoot, hiking up an uncertain old footpath with a load of camera equipment and having to contend with strong gusts of wind and the splashes of dust. He told of how at one point the wind had lifted his big view camera off its tripod as if it were a sprig of tumbleweed. At the last minute, he reached and grabbed the leg of the tripod just before the lens was about to come down on a jagged rock. Tapping his hand on this chest, he said, "It was like seeing my own child run in front of a car." He took a long swig of beer.

Stef was full of adrenalin. He looked at the zocalo and saw the beauty of San Miguel and its magic—the magic that Andy had described earlier that day. He stared at the buildings and the old cathedral. I could tell Stef was falling in love.

CHAPTER ELEVEN

June 12, 1980 – Day 11

Las Tortugas is a speck of a place—as Mexican as can be. A room made of thick stones and huge wooden beams across the ceiling and windows that opened onto the narrow street of Calle de Cinco de Mayo. A dark smoky room with a small bar and a dozen tables of old hardwood.

As soon as we came in, Andy Kozinsky was out of his chair and over to greet us. He introduced us to the others at the table. There was a painter named Gerry West who had an oval face and receding hair and ears that stuck out from his head—straight out. When he laughed, his mouth grew to twice its size. And he laughed a lot. I wondered what he painted. Clowns I figured, something like that. Gerry clutched a bottle of beer. He never took his hand off it the whole night, as though if he did it might float up into the air and out the window and down Calle de Cinco de Mayo, finally smashing against the side of the cathedral, spilling its contents onto the worn flagstones. Only when one bottle was empty did Gerry abandon it for another, and another, and another. I found some artistic continuity to all this—that even in a saloon this man, the artist, was fulfilling a need to touch his world. I liked that thought. Probably, though, he was just terribly nearsighted.

Then there was Miles, a poet, who looked to be about forty years old. He had a wide nose like a boxer's, and caramel eyes, and thick black hair that he tied behind his head. He was large, with big-crafted features, except for a shrunken left hand that he kept on his lap. He rarely moved it except once or twice during the evening. Then it came up like an exclamation point to emphasize a statement. Miles wore a poncho on top of a shirt, and this made him look larger yet. He must have been god-awful hot, I thought.

Andy told everyone of our plans to travel the Gringo Trail. Miles said it would be wonderful. Gerry agreed. "Do it now," he said, "Before it's ruined."

"It's too late. It's already been discovered," the woman sitting next to Andy contritely said. Her name was Chloe; it was evident she was with Andy. She had a simple and natural beauty— wonderful eyes, light brown hair, skin tanned dark as toast. She was so beautiful I had to try not to stare at her.

"Discovered, perhaps, but not ruined," Andy claimed. "There's still time to see it as we did."

"Yes, true, if you go now," said Gerry. "But it's changing fast…too fast. Soon the Trail will be a superhighway with Holiday Inns and T-shirt shops out in the jungle. And people will sell little plastic figurines of Mayan art. And, of course, lots and lots of tourists in Bermuda shorts."

"True…someday that will happen," said Andy. "But for now there's still a hell of a lot of jungle. Washed out roads and rickety old buses that break down every fifteen kilometers, always in the thick of things. Remember how it was?" he said, turning to Chloe.

"Stef's a photographer." He gave Stef a wink. "You'll get your chance to shoot. Just wait." I could almost hear Stef's heart race.

Now the room was full of people. A man sat at a rustic piano in the corner of the room. He played love songs, singing softly, sometimes in English, sometimes in Spanish. A ceiling fan moved the smoky air in foggy currents, chasing some of it out the window into the dark street.

Now and then a Mexican passing by would stop and peer in the window before heading off into the night again. Everyone was friendly, though Miles, the poet, was very quiet. Little by little he began talking to me. He was from Gary, Indiana, from an area near the steel mills called Milltown.

"I have generations of steel in my blood," Miles said. "My father's a steelworker and my grandfather was a steelworker. My two brothers are in the mill and my sister's married to a foreman. I'd probably be there too, except for this." He lifted his left hand.

I talked to Miles and whenever I could I caught a glimpse of Chloe. Sometimes Gerry West joined our conversation, but mostly he just drank beer and leaned back in his chair and whistled to the songs from the piano. Gerry seemed diffuse. He would look around the table and smile with that wide-open grin of his. In no time, Stef and Andy were like old friends, joking and laughing and drinking. Chloe was right there with them. The room was hot. Miles, I thought, must be cooking inside all the clothes.

I finally gave in. "Aren't you hot in all that?"

He said he was very comfortable. "Watch the Mexicans. They wear long-sleeved shirts and shawls and ponchos all day. It keeps the heat out, not in."

That didn't make sense to me, but what he said about the Mexicans was right, so I assumed it must be true.

All the people in Las Tortugas seemed to know each other, and Andy seemed to know everyone. Now and then, he talked to a group at the table next to us. No one entered Las Tortugas who didn't immediately wave to Andy. Sometimes he would get up and go over and speak to them or bring them back to meet Stef and me.

In time, the wooden table in front of us was cluttered with empty beer bottles. The man at the piano banged away at the keys and the room grew hot and loud and steamy. At the table behind us, people started talking loudly. Two men were yelling at each other and a woman at the table was yelling at both of them, telling them to stop yelling. One of the men snapped up from his chair and grabbed the other man and pulled him across the table. Beer bottles flew onto the floor. The woman screamed. All at once Las Tortugas was quiet as a cave. As the two men tussled, one of them slammed his fist into the face of the other. Andy leaped from his chair and tried to peel the two apart, all the time yelling, "Fletch! *Fletcher! Cut it out! Dammit! Cut it out! Do you hear me? Cut it out.*"

Miles, who when he stood up was as big as a man could be, rushed to help Andy. He stood over the two men down on the floor. Reaching out with his good right hand, he grabbed Fletcher by the back of his shirt and all but lifted him off the ground and flung him against the wall. The man on the ground crawled to his knees and spat blood.

By now the Mexicans who worked at Las Tortugas were on

the scene. Luis, the bartender, was talking very fast and pointing at Fletcher. I barely caught a word of what he said. Fletcher told Luis to fuck himself and then stormed out. The other man left with the woman. Within minutes, Las Tortugas was back to its normal, laughing, steamy, hot, music, beer, tequila self.

A young Mexican boy, a working child who sold packages of gum in the streets of San Miguel, stood at the window watching all this. He stared into the wild, weird, crazy world of Las Tortugas with eyes as big as a desert moon. Then he turned to the street, and I heard his high voice fade into the night, "*Cheek-lay, cheek-lay, cheek-lay…*"

Luis came to our table with a plate of taquitos and a bowl of guacamole and a basket of tortilla chips. He thanked Andy and Miles for stopping Fletcher. Andy and Luis talked in Spanish, spitting out words very fast. Luis asked Andy to keep Fletcher out of Las Tortugas. Andy said he had no control over Fletcher. Luis pleaded for Andy's help, then he thanked Andy and Miles and went back to the bar.

Gerry, the painter, was quiet through all this. He seemed totally unconcerned and completely amused by what had happened. Finally he said, "Fletcher's left hook is getting better."

"Fletcher's a madman," Chloe said.

"He's a drunk," Andy explained. "He used to be a writer. A pretty good writer. But now he's drunk day and night. For a while when I first came here, we were good friends."

"It's sad," Miles said. "Nobody can help Fletcher. We've all tried a thousand times."

"He doesn't want help," Chloe insisted. "I have no sympathy

for him."

"Me either," said Gerry.

Late that evening when things were winding down, Stef leaned over to me. "I love this place, Alex. I love San Miguel. I could live here forever. I feel inspired. My blood's boiling. I know I did some good work today. I can feel it. Oh, I can feel it."

Stef and I walked through the dark streets of San Miguel to the edge of town where our tent was pitched. I spread my bedroll on the hard ground and sunk into a numb white sleep.

I awoke almost four hours later in exactly the same position as when I fell asleep. I was shaking all over, drenched in a cold chill. I looked at Stef. He was wrapped in his sleeping bag, eyes flickering like a dog's, deep in sleep. He was warm and comfortable. I opened my backpack and put on every piece of clothing I had: two pairs of pants, two shirts, a sweater, a jacket, and my rain poncho, and climbed back under the blanket. I was barely warm.

CHAPTER TWELVE

June 13, 1980 – Day 12

B y seven o'clock the sun was full and ripe and the inside of our tent was choked with heat. Stef looked at me.

"You all right, Alex?" he asked.

"No, man," I said. "I froze my ass off last night. Look what I had to do to keep warm." I peeled off clothes. "I put on everything I had and I still froze…out in the middle of the goddamn desert in the middle of Mexico."

The morning was slow. We spent most of it in the café. The day was beautiful; the desert heat warmed my brittle frosted bones. I was like a lizard seized by the warmth. We had orange juice and ate sweet bread and drank bittersweet Mexican coffee.

An old man came down the street by the café with an oxcart full of fruit—pineapples and mangos and papayas—destined to the market. He stopped in front of our table and talked to a woman with a child. I heard him say he had come from the train station where he had gathered his wares. Soon the street was choked with traffic, snarled by the old man's cart. People from everywhere began shouting at him, but it made no difference. He just stayed, immovable, until he had finished talking. Then, with a gigantic yank on the rope, the oxen trudged onward.

In the afternoon, Stef took off again for the sacred hills with his cameras and a canteen of water and a half dozen tortillas. I sat in the zocalo and read. It was so warm it made me drowsy.

Miles, the poet, walked across the zocalo wearing his poncho, his hair back behind his head. He saw me sitting on the bench and came over. He was going to his flat.

"Come along," he offered.

We walked up Avenida Independencia, turned into an alley, and entered a sunny bright courtyard filled with plants and trees. A girl, an American I think, was sunbathing naked in the court-yard.

"That's Virginia," Miles said, "beautiful, but lots of trouble. I stay clear of her. She's a student at the Instituto de Allende. Lots of trouble."

Trouble, yes, but was she worth it? I thought.

Miles unlocked the door to his flat. Inside, out of the sun, the rooms were cool. The house was sparsely but adequately fur-nished—lots of books, a desk, a couple of good chairs. There were paintings on the wall, beautiful paintings. I looked at one and saw the name G. West at the bottom. These were done by Gerry, the painter with the gaping smile and the billboard ears from last night. The paintings were not of clowns at all. They were a kind of modern-day impressionism, and they were as fine as anything I had ever seen.

One painting was particularly beautiful. It looked out over San Miguel down a narrow street towards the zocalo. Off in the distance was the cathedral; everywhere yellow sun splashed across the frescoed buildings. It was perfect. There was even a dog piss-ing against one of the old stone buildings the way some of the Re-naissance painters had done in their paintings. You had to look hard to see this because it was off toward the edge of the painting, but it was there.

"Gerry's a damn good painter," Miles said. "In my book, the best in San Miguel. And there are a hell of a lot of painters in San Miguel."

I walked across the room. Mile's desk was a giant high-rise of papers surrounded by a mountain of books. Above his desk, a short poem was stuck to the wall.

> entropy is
> ruining
> my life
> one damn day
> at a time

I had to laugh. Miles declared it to be the truest thing he ever wrote. He talked about his family in Gary, Indiana, saying they never understood him down here in Mexico, some sort of bum writing poetry. A man works for a living, Mile's father had once said. You sweat and when you sweat you know you've done an honest day's work, not scribbling "nursery rhymes" on paper.

"I published seven books of poetry," Miles said. "More than fifty of my poems have appeared in magazines, and I've won eight awards for poetry. I teach at the Instituto de Allende, the main art school here in Miguel, and I'm a visiting lecturer at three American universities. This fall I'm teaching a course at the University of Arizona. But none of my family ever read a word I wrote. Years ago I sent them a copy of my first book of poems. Then, months later when I was back in Gary, I went to the basement to get some old newspapers to put on the floor inside the back door because it was snowing. There in the stack of newspapers was my book of poems, still in the envelope—opened but probably not read. After that, I never sent anything more. It's tough, but I just accept it. I can't blame them, though. To them poetry is nothing more than graffiti on the walls in the locker room at the mill. That's what they associate it with. It doesn't really matter now. I would probably have been a poet no matter what. For years I used to think it was because of my arm, you know, but that's really not it. I worked just as hard being a good poet as my father did being a good foreman. But he can't grasp that."

A photograph was pinned to the wall next to Miles's desk. He saw me glance at it.

"That's Catherine," Miles said, with a shrug. "An old flame…she's gone now."

That, too, seemed difficult for Miles. I sensed something in Miles that was pure and true and yet unfulfilled. If anything, Miles's life (and Miles the person) was direct and expressive and open—uncomplicated—and yet like his hand, flawed. There were times when he seemed troubled, as if his life itself were a poem. The poet perhaps unable to separate what is from what should be. The quest for something better, and the inability to accept something less. Where is that line? When do we say, 'This is the way it is, there is no more'? Do we ever say that? When is life a poem and when is it not? If a poem is not perfect, how can life be perfect? This was the person I saw.

Miles said his friends in Miguel were the best people he ever met and that Andy was the world's answer to kindness and sincerity. He said Andy had gotten ripped off by everyone before he came to San Miguel because he trusted the whole world. But the little world of San Miguel is different. It's small and you're all alone in the vast desert.

"In a way we're pioneers out here," Miles said. "We depend on each other. If you fuck with people, pretty soon they'll fuck you back. And so the bad ones never stay long. There's no place for them to hide in Miguel."

We left the apartment and walked through the courtyard where Virginia was still basking, now toasting her front side. In a café by the zocalo, Miles told me about his experiences with mind states and meditation. He described the mind as existing in one of five levels called beta, gamma, alpha, theta, and delta. He said most of the time our mind operates in beta or gamma. Beta is a heightened state of awareness. Gamma is even higher. There, we can have bursts of insight, but it also can be a state of disorganized and frenetic mental activity. Alpha is a state of relaxed mental awareness used for problem solving and contemplation. Theta is deep relaxation, meditation. Then, finally, there's delta, the lowest mind state of all. We are in delta when we are asleep.

Miles said most people can achieve alpha naturally without making a conscious effort to do so, but the ultimate is theta or even delta. Delta is infinite and limitless, so it is impossible to fully experience all of delta. In delta the mind is totally calm and completely separated from the physical world.

"See, the mind is not a physical thing, it is contra-physical. It only exists in the body for the sake of the body. The body needs the mind, but the mind—the *spiritual* mind—doesn't need the body. The mind has no physical parameters. We put limits on our mind; we teach it to do less than it is capable of."

Miles explained that, in delta, the mind exists independent of the body. We can explore everything—life, art, love, science, the universe. Our minds become uneducated and are free to roam, to think, to create. In delta and theta, distance is irrelevant. Two people can come together mentally from thousands of miles apart in a matter of seconds. It is here that we think our purest thoughts. Our mind is opened creatively to the energy of the universe. We can use that energy even when we are in beta or gamma.

Miles told me some people get to alpha through meditation but meditation is not necessary for alpha. Alpha is quite different from the experience of meditation because it's more involved with what' happening in the present—life here on Earth.

"Thinking just about the wheel of a car will not get you to understand what an automobile is. But in understanding the whole car, you will appreciate the wheel," Miles said. "People don't like this because they reject the notion that we are capable of understanding highly complex things. That only people like Einstein or Richard Feynman, those people, the big geniuses, can do it. But it defeats the whole purpose of utilizing every aspect of our mind."

Miles said that most things in life are part physical and part mental, like making love, for example. "There are limits as to what we can do to enhance the physical enjoyment. But our state of mind has no restraint. The more we enhance it, the more the physical pleasure is increased."

We sat at the café. I listened to Miles for a long time. I told him about my 'beta-gamma' world back in Baltimore. How I had been pushed—forced by the expectations placed on me and by my own expectations—to work at levels that defeated my goals of scientific discovery. But all that was changing in the short time I had been in Mexico; I was getting closer to alpha. I wanted to go all the way to theta and delta.

Late in the afternoon, Stef returned from the hills, again sweaty, hot, and happy. He sat at the café with Miles and me and ordered a drink. A while later Andy and Chloe joined us. We stayed there, talking, until long after sunset.

CHAPTER THIRTEEN

July 3, 1980 – Day 32

The next morning at around eight o'clock, Andy came to our camp. He asked Stef if he wanted to make a hundred dollars. "A friend called this morning from New York. He needs a short article with a couple of photos."

Minutes later, Stef's things were packed and he and Andy were heading down the dusty road that leads out of San Miguel. I went to the café, my permanent habitat for mornings, and penned another long letter to Maureen, telling her I missed her more than I ever expected. I wanted to tell her this again and again. When I was in Baltimore I never knew if I loved Maureen. I told her how I had taken this simple thing, life, and made it so damn complicated. I had ruined a good broth by trying to make a stew and in the end I didn't know what I had or what I started with. It was all a colossal mess. I tried to get to alpha and ended up back in gamma because all the people I believed in didn't know any better than I how to get to alpha. Now, I could start again. I knew this time I would get there. I knew Maureen wouldn't understand much about what I was saying, but I still had to say it. I told her for the first time ever how deeply I felt about her, and I meant it. I signed it:

With love, Alejandro.

Stef spent the afternoon processing film and printing in the darkroom at the Instituto de Allende. He gave Andy his photos and Andy delivered a hundred dollars for the work. In one short day, Stef had become part of the cadre of working artists in San Miguel. I knew it would be difficult, if not unfair, to expect him to pick up and leave. I knew he knew this too. Yet I was also aware that soon we would have to face that dilemma.

The next day, Andy found another job for Stef, this time for sixty dollars, a photo for a magazine in Mexico City. In two days, Stef had made a hundred and sixty dollars, a hell of a lot of money for the average person in San Miguel.

We sat at the café after Stef had returned from his second trip to the darkroom. It was a wonderful glorious afternoon, much cooler than the previous days—cool and balmy. We talked briefly. Soon, Stef said, "You about ready to leave San Miguel?"

I was surprised. "What do you mean? What do you want to do, Stef?"

"I'm gonna do what you want to do," Stef said.

"But there's so much here for you in San Miguel."

"But not for you, Alex. Not really."

"Well I can't ask you to leave because of me. I can go out alone."

"And I can't ask you to stay because of me. We'll go together." Stef ordered two ice-cold beers. It was settled.

We stayed in San Miguel for two more days. I spent most of that time at Miles's house or sitting with him in the café learning everything I could about mind states. He taught me more about how to get to theta—where to start and what to do. I stored each detail away in my mind as though burying a precious stone to be recovered at some time in the future. My soul was flushed with the expectation.

Stef photographed everything in San Miguel. He was up with the sun and out into the city stealing shots of the merchants and the vendors and the poor beggars up and down the skinny streets of San Miguel.

We spent our last night at Las Tortugas with Andy and Chloe and Miles and Gerry the painter. It was every bit as good as our first time. Fun and happy and perfect. Very late, we said goodbye and reluctantly headed off to our part of the city. Stef was unusually quiet. None of the buoyant energy that usually bubbled from him after a night like the one we just had.

As we walked through the drowsy streets of San Miguel, Stef said, "Someday, Alex, someday I'm coming back to Miguel. I don't know exactly when, but…I'll be back."

"I know you will, Stef," I said. "You should."

By the time I awoke the next morning, Stef was already up. He had made coffee and had filled his pack. We ate a breakfast of fruit and bread and then broke down the tent and talked a little about the weather. It was a beautiful day. Stef said he was feeling sort of queasy, sort of ragged inside—something from the water probably. We took our time getting things together and then set out on a slow hike to the railroad station outside San Miguel.

When we arrived at the station, I asked about the train to Mexico City. I was told it would come at eleven o'clock. I bought two tickets. Stef's spirits seemed to have improved. He started playing a game of soccer with some of the rag-tag children who lived near the train station. They set up our packs as goal posts and the kids tried to score as Stef stood between the packs. After fifteen minutes, Stef was dripping with sweat. Pale, as though all life had been sucked from his body. He gave up the net and slumped against the wall of the station. I asked how he felt. "Sick," he said. I told him to sit down, for Christ's sake, relax…take it easy.

Eleven o'clock came and went without a train—then twelve o'clock passed. I asked the ticket agent when the train would arrive.

"Eleven o'clock," he said.

"But it's twelve o'clock now," I said.

The man shrugged and went about his business.

I went outside and walked a ways up the railroad tracks. I remembered reading that somewhere in this very stretch of tracks, little more than a decade earlier, Neal Cassady had fallen unconscious in a drunken stupor, and later died. Neal Cassady, who modeled the legendary Dean Moriarty in Jack Kerouac's classic novel *On the Road*. I walked back to the station where Stef still leaned obliquely against the building.

"What time's the train coming?" Stef moaned.

"Nobody knows," I said. "An old man told me not till three or four maybe. He said it had derailed."

"Now what?"

"Back to Miguel and get a bus."

Down the road again into town. Hot damn road in the open afternoon sun. But we were in luck. A car whizzed past, slammed on its brakes, and backed up. "Get in," the man said. He drove us right up to the bus station.

Within twenty minutes, we were barreling through the desert south of San Miguel. The bus was smaller and older and dirtier than any so far. Stef sat and looked straight ahead until we were far from San Miguel. Much too difficult to look back and see Miguel, sweet Miguel, fade behind us like a vanishing mirage.

The bus stopped in the village of Queretaro. I remembered this as Jose Ramirez's village. We didn't stay long, but I knew it must be a good town if Jose was from there. Out onto the dusty highway, the bus hummed onward. The sun set over a ridge of low mountains to our right. Soon, the sky burst into flames of orange and red and purple and the sun was gone and the desert was cool. Stef and I talked about many things and, most of all, about San Miguel. It's hard to leave a lover.

By nine that night, the bus was squeezing its way through the barrios on the outskirts of Mexico City. A shantytown. Shacks of corrugated steel and cardboard. A pitiful statement to mankind in the twentieth century. Mile upon mile of this. One bare hut after another and another. In the doorway, a child stood with another small child in her arms. Next to her, people sat on old thin chairs under the gloom of Mexico City. Men, women, children, all living in tin cans. Then finally, out of the barrios and in the city—a big, bold, busty city. So damn big. Too damn big. Our bus chugged down one dark street after another until at last it crept helplessly into a grimy bus station. We got off and looked around.

"Now what?" I asked.

"Get the hell out of this place," Stef demanded.

We opened our map.

"We can go to Puebla," I said. "It doesn't look far. A hundred kilometers maybe. And that will take us out toward the Yucatan. We can probably still get to Puebla tonight."

I checked at the ticket window; there were no buses leaving for Puebla. Instead we had to get across town—across the world—to another station. A young Mexican girl told us for a peso we could take the subway to get there. And so, hot and tired, with Montezuma chasing us, we took off into the dark sick night of Mexico City.

After a couple of blocks, we came upon the entrance to the subterranean tunnel of the subway. We walked down the steps into the bowels of the city. God knows what we'd find there! I went to put a peso in the turnstile when suddenly a guard rushed over and started roaring at us in Spanish.

"What's he saying?" Stef asked.

"You're *not* going to believe this," I drolled, "but it's against the law to ride the subway with a backpack."

Stef stared at me with pallid eyes.

I said it again: "It's against the law to ride the subway with a backpack."

We turned and trudged back up the steps to the toxic city streets.

"What a god-damned law," Stef mumbled. "In a city where people live in tin cans."

We flagged a taxi and went across town to the bus station and finally, for the first time in Mexico City, we were in luck. We climbed aboard a bus just as it was ready to leave for Puebla.

The ride to Puebla was short; I slept for part of it. In Puebla all we wanted was a good room and a comfortable bed. We'd been up for days it seemed. As we walked down an empty street toward the plaza, a drunk zigzagged in our direction, swaying on shaky legs. He stopped about fifty feet from us and planted himself squarely in the street, leaned back and pissed in the middle of the road. Welcome to Puebla!

We found a hotel near the plaza and rented a room. From outside, the hotel looked nice, but I didn't like the desk clerk with his funny smile, particularly at one o'clock in the morning.

We went up to our room on the second floor. A dirty room with a broken window open to an alley and a seedy mattress and an unclean toilet. I didn't like the looks of the room, or the hotel, or anything about it, so I wedged a chair against the door. Then I fell asleep—far, far away.

CHAPTER FOURTEEN

July 4, 1980 – Day 33

In the morning we washed up and took our packs and left the hotel and went to the plaza where we sat at one of the sidewalk cafés near the square. Puebla is famous for its ornate Mexican tiles, and the entire city, inside and out, is decorated with these around the windows and doorways of the old stone buildings. The zocalo was beautiful, teeming with palm trees and flowers and tropical plants. I felt better sitting outside—rested and again ready for whatever was in store. Stef said he was wiped out. That he couldn't look at food; it made things rumble inside him.

"We can stay here a few days. It's not such a bad place," I said.

Stef promptly rejected that.

"I think you're just sick. Nothing looks good when you're sick," I said.

"I don't feel so bad," Stef said. "I just don't want to stay here."

"We can get a better place than what we had last night."

Stef shook his head. "I'm ready to leave."

"Okay, we leave." I took out our map and stretched it across the café table. Heading east toward the Yucatan, the next village was Orizaba. After that, Vera Cruz—sitting at the bottom of the Gulf of Mexico. The Gateway to the Yucatan.

"And no more fucking buses," Stef said. "We use our thumbs today. Can't take any more rickety buses."

I ate breakfast and had coffee. We tied our packs and headed for the edge of town. Though barely ten o'clock, the temperature was pushing a hundred. White sun up in a big cloudless sky. We walked for a mile down a road that led into the desert, trying to pull a ride. But the infrequent and indifferent cars just whizzed past. Stef clumped ahead, his back to the traffic, his left hand and thumb up in the air. We walked for an hour or so. My mouth, my skin, my eyes were dry as clay. A white Volkswagen minibus pulled off the road next to me. I thought it might be stopping for repairs, but as I walked by, the driver said, "A donde va?"

"Down the road." I pointed straight ahead. *Just anywhere*, I thought, *anywhere out of this sun*. "Where are you going?" I asked. But before he could answer, before he could think of an excuse, I said, "Can we get a ride?"

The driver, a Mexican in his early twenties, looked at me. He looked at Stef, marching ahead on the highway. I tried to get Stef's attention. I called and yelled, but he kept plodding straight ahead like a robot. At the same time, I didn't want to lose the ride, so I talked to the driver, giving him no chance to think about all this— these two sunburned Gringos with their gypsy rucksacks.

A carfull of Mexicans sped past us. People in the back seat tried to signal to Stef, as if to say, "Look, there's a ride, you nut."

Finally, Stef turned, saw me and the van, and came charging back in full gallop. I kept talking to the man and just about the time Stef got to the minibus, the driver said, "Okay, si, vamanos."

We threw our packs into the van and climbed aboard. Once again we were rolling through the sandy dusty desert to nowhere.

The diver's name was Trinidad. He was from Mexico City and worked for a company that delivered dairy equipment to rural towns and little isolated villages all over Mexico. He worked for three weeks at a time driving in a huge arc from Mexico City to Vera Cruz to Monterrey and back to Mexico City. Then he got a week off. And then started over again. He said he had a wife and a two-year-old daughter back in Mexico City and that he made good money on this job—thirty-five dollars a week. I wondered if he lived in one of those tin cans back in the big city.

"Where are you going?" Trinidad asked again.

"To the Yucatan," I said.

"We want to get to Orizaba today," Stef said.

Trinidad looked at both of us and started laughing. "Orizaba is that way, amigo," he said, pointing out the window to his left. "This road goes south to Tehuacán." He talked mostly in Spanish, then in English he said, "You meeesed the highway, man."

"Can we get to Orizaba from here?" I asked.

"Oh yes, but it will take a while. The road goes all over."

"How long?"

"Long time…not today, that's for sure." He couldn't help laughing at the two Gringos, the two lost and loco Gringos he had come across out in the desert.

I looked at Stef and then out at the vast empty world around us. I said, "Well, Trinidad, we go to Tehuacán with you then."

Trinidad smiled and, in his best broken English, said, "Okay, amigos, we go to Tehuacán."

We crashed on through the desert—Trinidad drove good and hard. Stef was feeling better now. He leaned back in the seat with the top of his head out the window as he had done when we'd rolled through the Mississippi lowlands. He started singing songs just like back then. Trinidad bounced up and down in his seat, leaning forward and tapping his hand against the steering wheel. He started singing songs in Spanish—old Mexican love songs. I sat in the middle between him and Stef. I had no idea where we were going and I didn't care.

We barreled across the desert for hours, through the noonday sun and into the blistering afternoon. The temperature blasted up to a hundred and twenty or a hundred and thirty and the air was dry as a broken twig. There was nothing out in the desert, not even the lonely little huts we'd seen in the parched land of northern Mexico. A big white desert full of white sand with a blistering sun splashing down on us.

The two-lane highway was an empty stretch of road—one or two cars all afternoon. How would we have survived out there alone, I wondered, on this abandoned road going nowhere through an empty world?

We drank all the water we had, and that was in the shade of Trinidad's van. How could we have survived in the open sun with no place for shade? But Trinidad had plenty of water that he shared freely with us. He carried two huge jugs with him in case he broke down in the desert.

"What would you do if that happened?" I asked.

"It did…twice," he said. "I just sit inside and wait. Sooner or later someone comes along. But once I had to wait for a whole day."

About two o'clock, Trinidad reached behind the seat and pulled out a brown bag with a bottle of tequila. He held it up and proudly said, "Do you like?"

Stef laughed. What a welcomed sight in this desert of desolation. Trinidad uncorked the bottle and freed the magic spirits. We passed the bottle around again and again. The lightning from the cactus trapped in the bottle raced through my body, turning switches on and turning switches off. Now the open empty desert took on a new look. I wondered where we were. Not just in what desert, but where in the whole damn universe? If I was lost in the desert, was I lost in the universe? I asked aloud, "Where the hell are we?"

Trinidad simply said, "En Me-hi-co."

It wasn't the answer I wanted but it was at least an answer.

Stef sat quiet for a while. Then he started singing again, this time wailing the blues in a low gastric voice. He sang songs by The Doors:

> *Well, I've been down so goddamn long,*
> *That it looks like up to me.*

Stef hallooed one deep dark chorus after another, the Lost-in-the-Desert Mexico Blues.

Trinidad bounced. He shouted, "Oh! Yes! Yes! Ees The Doors!" He started singing "LA Woman," every word perfect beginning to end. We all sang the blues. That's what I like about the blues. They'll get you through anything. And so we sang the blues. And more Doors. And Mexican love songs. All of it blasting out of the window of Trinidad's van into the hard hot earth that surrounded us.

The desert was low and flat and smooth as the ocean. It seemed to be endless, past today, into tomorrow, and through the future—everything trapped in the desert. We drove on and on but went nowhere. The desert moved around us as we stood still. Finally, after hours of this, up ahead far off in the distance I saw the vague outline of a massive lone mountain. Gigantic mountain. Too perfect to be a mountain, it was like a pyramid.

"What's that, Trinidad?" I asked.

"Es Pico de Orizaba."

"A mountain?" Stef asked.

"A bal-cano," Trinidad replied.

Pico de Orizaba—eighteen thousand feet tall—the third tallest peak in North and Central America.

Stef sat straight up and just kept saying, "Wow" and "Would you look at that."

Trinidad said Pico was his friend, that they were both alone out there in the desert. He told us volcanoes keep away evil spirits and make the desert safer.

Trinidad hammered the van to eighty miles an hour down the center of the highway in a perfect straight line. At about five o'clock we arrived in the town of Tehuacán, a small oasis full of palm trees and pulpy green plants—a quaint subdued village known for the mineral water that's sold all over Mexico.

We drove into Tehuacán twice as drunk from drinking all day

on an empty stomach with only Trinidad's water to chase away the cactus spirits. Trinidad took us to a hotel where we rented a room and then went to a restaurant and had dinner of tamales and rice and pinto beans and a whopping stack of soft steamy tortillas. I drank two huge bottles of Tehuacán mineral water—after all, we were in Tehuacán. Then, tired as a lizard on a hot rock, I went up to the room and slept.

CHAPTER FIFTEEN

July 5, 1980 – Day 34

We stood at the edge of a cliff facing a murky ravine. Brown pungent smoke sifted up from a hole and an oppressive heat swirled around us. Behind us was a forest of some kind, except that the trees were squat and mushy. They had no leaves, only pulpy finger-like projections. Everything was vague and obscure. Something nearby breathed foul bilious breath. Stef spoke to me, but I couldn't hear him. His mouth moved but no words came out. I tried to listen, but there was nothing to hear. The ravine vomited tarry vapors that clung to my throat like bloody mucus. From a bush, an enormous pterodactyl-like creature with the head of a monkey flew over the swamp and swooped towards me. Again and again it swooped down, each time closer. Each time the bird laughed in a shrill psychotic voice. Stef stood by, camera strung around his neck, rolls of film strung to the camera strap. He clicked the shutter as fast as it would go, shooting, shooting, shooting. I swung at the bird but fell into the soggy clay. The creature danced through the air over me.

When I awoke, my hands were clenched in tight fists and my

body was stiff and arched. I saw sunlight coming through the window. Stef and Trinidad were not around. I heard Stef washing up in the bathroom.

"Where the hell's Trinidad?" I called. "Did he leave without us?"

"No, no, he's downstairs," Stef answered.

I felt the way Stef had in Puebla. Weak and queasy.

After breakfast, we drove out of Tehuacán heading northeast into the mountains. Stef sat up front with Trinidad and I sat in back. We curled toward the sky on a twisty little road, higher and higher, back and forth through the mountains. Seven thousand, ten thousand, twelve thousand feet. The air was chilly and clean. Cows grazed along the hills. Corn sprouted against the vertical mountainside. But I saw no people. We slinked higher up the mountain.

Stef watched everything, camera by his side for the first time since San Miguel. Trinidad drove carefully up the fragile road, never going more than twenty-five or thirty miles an hour. An angelic silence fell over us, high above the desert, far from civilization.

I thought about Maureen. All my thoughts were pulled toward her as I concentrated on that one thought. I heard nothing from the world around me. My mind lifted me away from the little van on the side of the mountain in Mexico.

I closed my eyes and felt myself float far out into the cosmos—soaring, gliding through the stars into a long empty void, finally resting softly in perfect calmness. There I stayed for a long while. I saw the spirits of Maureen and my parents and my sister.

I could talk with everyone and they could talk with me. I learned that my cousin had been hurt at work, though not seriously, and that he had to stay home for a few days. And that my sister's oldest boy was the star of the little league team—he hit two home runs last week. And most of all, I learned that Maureen was happy, though suffering through a miserable Baltimore summer. She loved the letters and said to keep writing. She told me to be careful and safe and to keep an eye on Stef, and hurry back.

When I opened my eyes, the van was aimed sharply up the mountain, creaking along slow and steady. The road was raw and rutted. We bounced up and down and from side to side. I wondered how long we'd been doing this. In the front seat, Stef hung out the window, popping off frames. Trinidad's eyes were glued to the road, hands tight on the wheel. The air was cool and the sky was blue.

We sliced through low-hanging clouds as we went up the mountain. The land around us was green, not burned like the desert. The hills were speckled with patches of planted corn. For the first time since we started up the mountain, I saw a person, an old man walking along the road. He stopped and watched as our van sneaked past him. I saw his dark, brown, gnarled face.

Trinidad threw the van into low gear; we inched our way up like an ant on a brick wall, feeling each step. After a while, we turned off the road onto a flat dirt path that opened onto a valley high on the mountain. A jagged dirt road that led to an open stretch of rolling green mountain pasture. Up ahead was a village with a dozen or so adobe huts. We stopped at the village. Trinidad climbed out of the van. A man came from one of the huts and talked to him.

Soon the entire village appeared for the occasion. These were native Mexican Indians—there was not a drop of Spanish blood in any of them. They had dark skin and high cheekbones and hair that was straight and black.

It was cool in the mountains. Misty thin clouds sifted through the air. Each person wore a shawl or a poncho made of wool. Behind one of the huts, I saw sheep grazing with their own layer of thick wool. The Indians had come out to see Trinidad on his monthly visit. But immediately, Stef stole the show.

"You're a celebrity," I said. "Look, I think some of them have never seen blond hair."

Within minutes, the front of our van was surrounded by dozens of people squeezing in closer and closer to get a look at Stef. Only the old man talking to Trinidad seemed undistracted by Stef's presence—probably the only person in the entire village who'd ever been down the mountain.

Trinidad came around and opened the side of the van and unloaded equipment. He looked at Stef. "How are you doing, amigo?"

"I don't know, Trini, is everything okay here?"

"Oh, it's fine. These are good people."

One of the children reached inside the window and touched the back of Stef's head. She petted him as one would do to the hair of a doll. Then, suddenly, she pulled back and her eyes grew big as walnuts, startled by what she had done. Trinidad and the old man talked and laughed, watching what was happening. Pretty soon Trinidad finished unloading his deliveries. He climbed into the van and started backing out of the village. As we headed away, a woman ran up to the van with a heavy wool poncho and stuck it inside the window next to Stef. Stef looked at Trinidad and said, "What's this for?"

"It's for you," Trinidad said.

"I can't take this."

"You have to."

Stef stared at Trinidad.

"You have to," Trinidad said, again. "If you don't the whole village will be hurt."

Stef took the poncho from the old woman and said, "Gracias." He looked out at the rest of the people and waved and said, "Gracias, amigos."

As we pulled out of the village back to the mountain road, Trinidad said, "It's easy to see how Cortez with a few hundred soldiers conquered Montezuma's army of two hundred thousand."

We stopped at three more villages. At each one, people gathered around our van and stared at Stef. The villages were small and simple. We were not just high above civilization; we were out of civilization. There were no telephones, no electricity, no drugstores, no hotels or restaurants. No banks, paved streets, streetlamps, gas stations. No cars.

We left the last village and rode again into the mountains—mountains as somber and peaceful as the seashore. We were up so far from the world, so high above its tin can cities, so far from its silly subways, from its scruffy-hot deserts, its dirty buses and derailed trains. That was all below us as we pulled through the mountains with Trinidad—courier to the Indians, link to the past. *We don't belong up here*, I thought. This was the last place for the Indians, chased high into the sky, pushed up the mountains by a world they were not part of.

I realized we had come into the past, or perhaps the past had come to us, to Stef and me riding in Trinidad's time machine. Somewhere below, the present existed with all its crazy frenzied energy, crashing into the future with the grace of a tornado. I felt a great peace come through me. It soaked into my skin and muscle and bone and blood, through my whole body. A perfect calm came over me. I noticed and sensed everything around me. We weaved through the mountains for an hour or so. Dusk came and the sun set to our left, a silver sunset up above the world.

"This is where I usually spend the night," Trinidad said. "There are no more villages until we get down the mountain."

We pulled off the road onto a patch of thick green grass. Stef set up our tent. I gathered wood and built a fire. Trinidad had some eggs and bacon and birotes and tortillas, and we cooked up a grand meal. I boiled water and made coffee. The weather turned cooler and cooler after the sun set. I put on a long-sleeved shirt and a sweater. Stef wrapped himself in his new poncho. A big down-to-the-knees poncho that still bore the smell of sheep's wool. We talked for a while and Trinidad told us about Mexico City. He loved Mexico City. Stef and Trinidad talked, but all I wanted to do was drink from the river of peace that flowed around me.

We slept.

I was up with the sun. So simple, this mountain—pure and perfect, full of life. I wondered why I was here. I didn't know the answer. Perhaps it was the wrong question. The old mountain told me nothing, though I knew it had answers. I knew all answers exist. It's part of the balance of Nature. If there is a question, there is an answer. I had to find the answers.

By mid-morning, we were in the van and angling down the mountain as a warm sun broke over us. One last stop for Trinidad that morning. But a good stop indeed, with time for a cup of local mountain coffee and a sweetbread for each of us. Farther on down the mountain to where things looked more and more like the world I knew. Out onto the highway, speeding toward Orizaba.

CHAPTER SIXTEEN

July 6, 1980 – Day 35

Orizaba is not much of a town—plain and simple and rather unattractive. A lot like some small towns in Texas, Mexican style. Trinidad had at least day's work there before he started off again. We said goodbye at the bus station and he headed back to the highway, waving until he was out of sight.

We walked into the station and checked about a ticket to Vera Cruz. The station was a rat hole of people bumping against each other. It was a wretched place. I don't know if it was really that bad or it just seemed so after coming from the mountain. Funny to think the Indians up there were being denied all this. We stood in a slow line, waiting to get a ticket. The person in front of us, a tall fair-haired man with a copy of Tolkien's *Hobbit* wedged into his back pocket, turned and looked at us. "Where're you going?"

"To Vera Cruz, assuming we can get a ticket," Stef replied.

"Hah…don't take the bus, take the train," he said.

"We tried the train once, but it never came," I replied.

The man smiled. "They're unpredictable. But more often than not they're worth the wait. Especially the one going to Vera Cruz from here. You won't believe what you'll see."

"What do you mean?" I asked.

"You'll see when you ride the train." He added, "After all, what could be worse than this, right?"

He had a point.

He told us how to get to the train station and, almost as an order, said to wait until the train arrived—it was always late.

As in San Miguel, the train station was located on the edge of town. When we arrived, the station was all but empty. We studied the board above the ticket window and bought two tickets to Vera Cruz. The train would arrive at one o'clock. (Sure!)

We hung around the station. Soon people began to filter in. They gathered on the platform next to the tracks, watching Stef and me with great curiosity. An old man who worked at the station started talking to Stef. He introduced us to a younger man named Hector who worked for the railroad. I never quite found out what Hector's job was. Some sort of railroad inspector. But mostly he walked back and forth along the platform looking very macho. He pretended to be unimpressed by our presence, but this changed quickly when he learned we were from Baltimore. His face broke out of its cold hard stare. "Baltimore! You mean like the Baltimore Orioles?" He proceeded to name each player…and their batting averages…and the records they'd set. Everything. Once again Stef had pulled a friend out of the crowd.

Time passed, no train. Even Hector-the-Inspector didn't know when the train would arrive. The afternoon wore on. Two o'clock. Three o'clock. More people at the station. Lots of poor people with cardboard boxes wrapped and tied with rope—Mexican luggage. By four o'clock, the station was overrun with people. Finally, way off down the tracks, I could see the train coming, crawling along, creeping along. Cripes, I could walk faster than that. I wondered how all these people would fit on the train.

As it lumbered closer, I could tell it was already filled to the seams. People were hanging out windows and doors and even before it stopped people from the platform climbed on. Others handed boxes through the open windows. Hector grabbed Stef and me by the arm and pushed through the crowd, ordering people out of the way in the name of the railroad. It was sort of funny, but I felt embarrassed as he jolted aside lame old men and poor peasant women. When the train could take no more people, its wheels strained and it tiptoed out of the station and, even then, people scrambled on.

We stood in the area between two cars. Human cattle on a human cattle train. I looked into one of the cars. We were much better here, I thought, with lots of fresh air. The train was packed with people—peasants and Indians and children with dark eyes. The train creaked and rocked and gradually picked up speed. It shook from side to side in a fine regular rhythm. We were headed straight into the eastern coastal mountains of Mexico. The big city of Vera Cruz and the Gulf Coast lay on the other side. The train puffed and pulled and groaned its way through the jagged, high mountains—dark and green like the ones we had just come down from with Trinidad. For an hour or so we continued on a ribbon of rails that snaked around and up.

We arrived at the top of the mountain; everything changed. Within minutes we had come into a different world that, almost magically, was hot and humid and tropical. Moving into a deep verdant jungle, every speck of my skin began to sweat. My clothes stuck to my soggy body. I inched toward the door of the train. The jungle was full of painted birds and monkeys and fruit that hung loose from the trees. So green it was it seemed to be black. Everything was out of proportion—leaves were three feet wide, vegetation was so thick it grew right up to the side the train.

Stef stood close to the open train doorway, which was nothing more than a gaping hole into the jungle. He started to photograph the raw beautiful world around us, leaning out the door, holding on for his life with his left hand while working the camera with his right. His body pointed out the side of the car at forty-five degrees as we crossed over a bridge made of steel cables and tracks strung between two jungle mountains. Nothing below but a green forest two hundred feet down. The jungle burst with a million beautiful sights.

Stef worked as if in a trance, sweating rivers of perspiration. One of the peasants reached and grabbed him by the back of his belt, another held his left arm, and another reached and clung to his waist, making a lifeline. As they did this, Stef let go of the train and put both hands to work on his camera, hanging out the train, far out, his life now suspended in the hands of the peasants. More people grabbed onto Stef, some held his leg, another reached for his ankle.

I stood back and saw a pure and honest kindness in these people, their desire to help this odd-looking stranger. A part of me wondered where we had lost this. What had we accomplished by becoming self-sufficient packages, too often unwilling to rely on each other? The alternative seemed so much better. Stef pulled back into the train and reloaded his cameras. Sweat sprayed off his face. He was breathing fast in his adrenalin high. He looked at the peasants and smiled and they smiled at him. Loaded and ready, he dangled out the door once again. The peasants fought for a chance to cling to his leg or arm. Some even hung onto the people who hung onto Stef. The sun began to set and the jungle was full of shadows. At last, the light gave out and Stef climbed back in.

The jungle became dark and mysterious. Our train pushed on into the hot night. We rode for two hours between mountain peaks, then gradually started down toward the sea. A slow descent from high in the sky. Down and around until we leveled off onto flat ground. The train picked up speed. We passed poor shanty towns along the railroad. In the distance I saw the lights of a big city. Everyone on the train was up and moving about—picking up kids and packages and bags and suitcases.

Life on the outskirts of Vera Cruz was like on the edge of Mexico City. A dark abandoned world bubbling in the thick night. We pulled through a trainyard. I saw people living in boxcars. Whole families. Each car the same. Seven or eight people stuffed in. A table, a bare electric bulb, cots. People watched us as we shuttled past. Carloads of people. They had that same hollow, sad, nothing-else-to-do look I saw in Mexico City. But these were the real tin can people, and there was a whole village of them, living on rails but going nowhere, motionless, in perfect rows in the train yard. We passed this city-on-the-rails for a mile or so until the train lumbered to a stop at the Vera Cruz station.

CHAPTER SEVENTEEN

July 6, 1980 – Day 35

Our four-hour ride through an unknown world had brought us to the edge of Mexico on the lush sweeping Gulf. We walked out of the station and went to the center of town where a big zocalo greeted us—a full two blocks on each side with a broad park in the middle.

Old, white, Spanish-style hotels, each with a sidewalk café, faced the zocalo. Calypso bands tapped bongos and steel drums. The train ride, though short, was exhausting. We found a table at one of the cafés and ordered drinks. I watched the waiter deliver steamed shrimp to the table next to us. Big shrimp soaked in butter and garlic with a dab of chili powder. The smell of food overcame me; my mouth watered. We were both starving, not having eaten anything but a piece of sweetbread all day. A day that in some ways seemed three years long. Stef looked at the menu and checked the prices. We decided to treat ourselves to a platter of shrimp. Hot calypso music pulsed through the square.

We talked about the train ride. The man at the bus station in Orizaba had been right. The mountains were spectacular, much more than just a physical barrier through the eastern portion of Mexico. In every way, they divided different cultures. The people of Vera Cruz were unlike the people of the central deserts, just as people in Iowa or Nebraska differ from people in New York or Connecticut. Vera Cruz has a Caribbean soul. The heat and humidity brought a sultry sensuality to the city. The women were more beautiful and more seductive than any so far. They wore cool flower-print dresses, a fresh white flower in hair black as onyx. They walked by our table and looked at us, not with curiosity but with seduction. Stef was no novelty to these women—he was temptation.

Our dinner arrived. Nothing in my life tasted so good. It was a huge plate of delicious shrimp served with a small salad. After dinner we treated ourselves to coffee and a shot of Kahlua. I felt good but tired. We still had to find a place to spend the night. A person at the café told us about an area up the road near the beach where we could camp. He pointed the way. We started out on foot, walking for five or six blocks in the cruel heat. I stopped and set my pack down to catch my breath.

"It must be ninety-five degrees," I said. "If this were the desert, it'd be cool by now."

We walked far down a road that followed the shore of the Gulf. The more we walked, the more we dripped with sweat. The night seemed to be getting hotter, not cooler. We stopped again. I wiped my forehead with my shirt.

"Maybe we're going the wrong way," Stef said. "We walked for at least a mile."

"We can't turn around now. Let's keep going. We'll find something."

Farther down the road. Vera Cruz shrunk behind us. As hot a

night as I had ever known. It had been a day of wonderful new experiences, but now it was becoming an endless day, and I was miserably hot and tired. My body was full of a million aches and pains.

We walked along. I put my thumb out hoping for a ride. Cars whizzed by until finally a VW bug pulled to a stop. In it were three young Mexican girls with that black hair and those black eyes and that same seduction we'd seen in Vera Cruz.

"We're looking for a place to camp," I said, desperately.

"Si," said one of the girls. She pointed up ahead.

"Will you take us?" I asked.

She laughed.

We climbed in.

The girls looked at Stef, his hair stuck to his face. We looked like two rats caught in a flood, and we smelled. The girls smelled like flowers. They were clean and fresh and full of that Vera Cruz beauty. I asked what they were doing riding around like this. It was Sunday night, they said. Until then I had no idea what day it was. I sat in the VW and watched the sea with its silvery surf. I was captured by the thought that for the first time since I was a small child I didn't know or care what day it was. I didn't know the day of the week, or the day of the month. All of that, I had left somewhere behind—perhaps in the mountains, or in the jungle, or maybe in the back of Trinidad's van. It was gone now, and I didn't miss it one damn bit.

The VW stopped and the driver said, "This is it." She let us out, turned the car around, and whizzed back into the night.

In the morning, Stef was up early. I felt rested and better, but my body was as tight as a sailor's knot. Funny, though, it felt good that way.

A bus line ran down the highway by the camp into Vera Cruz. We went into the city.

The beaches along the highway were starting to fill with their daily worshippers. We got off the bus in Vera Cruz and walked around. Stef photographed the old buildings, and we went to the market as we always did in a good city. The market was wonderful and busy and even better than the one in San Luis Potosi. We walked back to the zocalo and sat in the shade of a cabana and ordered a licuado, a drink made of fresh fruit juice and crushed ice.

At the table next to us was another traveler sitting by himself. He began talking to us as soon as we arrived. He said he was from France, that his name was Tierry, and that he had traveled through the eastern US down to Mexico and out onto the Gringo Trail like us. He told us about his experiences. "When I was traveling in Tennessee, I tried to get a bus to Nashville. So, I said, 'I want to go to Nash-*ville.*' The bus man said, 'Well, I don't know where Nash-*ville* is. This here bus is going to *Na-a-a-a*-shville.' That's how they say it." Tierry repeated, "*Na-a-a-a*-shville."

Stef thought it was funny as hell—a pretty good imitation of a southern accent even with a French inflection.

Tierry didn't like Nashville, or most of the US for that matter. Too much fast food and no cafés. He didn't like Mexico either. Plenty of cafés but too dirty. And most of Mexico didn't like Tierry's arrogant look. He was big and tall and wiry and sort of funny looking. Stef immediately gave him the name "Nash."

We talked for a while. I could see Nash was tired of traveling alone. I could see all the good experiences were being lost because of nobody to share them with.

Would we be going to the Yucatan, he wanted to know. When would we be leaving? Could he travel with us for a while? What about these tortilla things? How come there was no bread down here? On and On. Nash told us where he was staying, and we said we were leaving Vera Cruz shortly, maybe tomorrow or the next day. We'd come and get him when we did.

We rode the bus back up to the campground and went out to the beach. It was crowded, but the water was warm and refreshing. We walked along the edge of the water looking at the Mexican girls in their bikinis. In the afternoon, we stopped at a stand and had another platter of shrimp. We sat in the shade of a big breezy palm and ate and drank ice-cold beer and watched the women. We would leave Vera Cruz in the morning; we wanted to get farther into the Yucatan.

"This Yucatan is a strange place, isn't it?" Stef said. "It's hot and miserable and tough and unforgiving. But it makes you want more."

Stef got that right.

He said, "The Yuke's like a real good woman, isn't it, Alex? The kind that makes you want more the badder she gets."

The next day we went into Vera Cruz and rounded up Nash and went to the bus station. Another urban blight. I found the line for tickets and took my place. Lord, what a line! Slow as a whisper. Lots of buses going east into the Yucatan. The next big city was Villahermosa. I stood in line for nearly two hours and then, just as I got to the ticket window, the man inside slammed down the shade. No more tickets. No more buses. "Mañana," he said as he shut the window.

I couldn't believe it. I wanted to scream and smash open the window and demand a ticket for all the crap he had put us through. All day, and now no buses. Nash went into a wild French frenzy. The Mexicans stopped and watched as he reeled off his anger in rapid French, thumbing his nose at the bus station and the ticket agent, and even at the Mexicans around him. We grabbed him by the arm, as he yelled frantically, and led him out of the station and went back to the hotel. In the morning we were on the first bus heading for the Yucatan.

Part Two

ISLANDS AND TROPICS

CHAPTER ONE

July 9, 1980 – Day 38

L ife was now one dilapidated bus after another—that's what it had become. Cheap little buses and old school buses with hard wooden seats packed with people. It seemed as though every other person had a long-necked chicken under his arm or in a basket, and every now and then one of these would stick its head out and take a snip at your arm. Nash hated it.

Dusty coastal road flat as Kansas. Blistering hot in the tropical sun in a bleached-out world. Bouncing through the Yucatan on a jagged rutted road in a bus with no springs. Lurching our way into the Yucatan at twenty-five and thirty and, oh Jesus, forty miles an hour! Tough old bus, as tough as the country itself.

We rode all morning and afternoon past the towns of Alvarado and San Andres Tuxtla and Coatzacoalcos. Across a low flat jungle that stretched out like blanket. A good hideaway for birds and animals and anything that doesn't want the touch of mankind.

Nash, tall and lanky, was miserable on buses made for Mexicans. He sat hunched in his seat with his knees to his chest, hands gripping the rail in front of him. Every minute or two as the bus took a dive into a rut, his body would uncoil and shoot up in the air. He moaned and all you could do was laugh to see him like this. At each stop he was up, crunching his way through the aisle to get off and stretch his legs.

We passed small insignificant towns, so we pushed on. Even Nash in his mortal misery wanted to keep moving. Now we were officially on the Gringo Trail—that sole, poor, pathetic path that sweeps around the perimeter of the Yucatan and down across Central America and back up again. Just as Andy had told us in San Miguel, the Gringo Trail is the only actual road into the Yucatan—most of the jungle being impenetrable—no roads, few towns.

We rode all day. As the night was setting in, there was a snap from the front of the bus; it tilted to the right and stopped on the edge of the jungle. The front tire had split apart. The bus emptied. The driver went about changing the tire. He pulled a good one from the top of the bus where there were eight or ten spare ones. He took the torn tire off and put it on top of the bus with the other busted ones. Nash was happy to be out of the bus. Stef climbed on top of the bus and took fruit and water and tortillas from our packs.

Soon, we were moving again, riding along at that endless pace. An hour later we stopped for another flat tire, and twenty minutes after that another yet. I calculated we still had five good spares left.

The sun vanished and the jungle was as black as the eyes of a Vera Cruz woman. There was nothing for me to do on the bus, wedged between a fat woman with her baby on my left and Stef on my right. Nash bounced on the seat across the aisle from us. As we rumbled through the jungle, I closed my eyes and thought about Maureen and wondered where she was at this very minute. What was she doing? Who was she with?

The bus plugged its way into the night. The Yucatan became still. We rode in the sheer stillness and suffered in the heat. I watched the driver. These buses were not like the big buses of northern Mexico, those luxury buses, where Jose Ramirez showed me the baggage compartment and the extra driver who rode in it. This bus was small, barely big enough to hold twenty people. It had only one driver, who sat at the wheel and aimed the bus into the black abyss. It must be a tough way to make living, I thought, driving a bus day in and day out, three or four flat tires on every trip. Guiding the poorest of the poor through Mexico from one coastal village to another in the hot steamy night.

A baby cried, then stopped as fast as it started. Again stillness. I tried to sleep and I did, I think, for a while. I let my head sink. My motionless body hung between the bodies of two other people, flesh stuck to wet flesh. Stef leaned against the window and slept for a while. I saw his head rap on the metal frame when we hit the bumps. Too tired to care. Again and again against the frame. Now, we were peasants.

I watched the sky that bloomed over the jungle. It was a carousel of spinning, shining, twirling stars. More stars than even in the desert. I felt as though we were being sucked into this thing, the Yucatan. Pulled in by its raw restless energy. Caught in some spinning vortex. Stef was right, what he said about the Yucatan, once you're in it, you can't leave. We were bugs near a fire.

Sometime deep in the middle of the night we pulled into Villahermosa. We had been riding for more than twenty hours only to arrive in the dirtiest, smelliest city I'd even seen. The bus station reeked and, even at three in the morning it was a clot of people. I was hungry, so I ate a taco from one of the vendors in the station. Meat of some kind in a tortilla. I was so hungry I ate two more. Stef had one and probed to see what he was eating. I told him to forget it, just eat. Nash couldn't watch.

"We have to get out of here!" Nash said. "This place is a toilet."

"Can we get a bus tonight, Alex?" Stef asked.

"To where?"

"Anywhere," Nash said. "I don't give a damn where. Anywhere at all."

"I don't know. I'm so damn hungry and so damn tired I don't know anymore," I said. "Maybe we can stay in Villahermosa, just for the night."

That caused an uproar. Nash and Stef both barked at me.

"Okay," I said, "Okay." I walked to the door of the bus station and peered into the street. Villahermosa was closed up tight and ugly. I came back and put my pack on the floor and sat on it and leaned against the building.

A bus pulled up and people poured into the station. A young woman about our age with a pack flung over her back walked up to us. We talked for a minute. She was Australian—petite, maybe five-one, but tough looking despite her size.

She peered intensely around the station. "Well, we're bloody well not staying here…are we?" She went over to the ticket window and talked to the man, half in English, half in Spanish, and came back. "Be damned if I'm hanging round till eight in the morning." She buzzed through the station three, four times, talking to the Mexicans. When she came back, she said, "C'mon, mates, we're going to another bus depot."

She slung her pack on her back and led us out of the station into the dark streets of Villahermosa. We followed in single file. She talked nonstop in a sharp Australian accent, telling us where she'd been—almost everywhere—and where she was going—everywhere she hadn't been. Her name was Yvette. What was ours? Where had we been? Where were we going? This is a bloody rotten town, isn't it? She was so charged with energy I thought she was pumped full of amphetamines.

"Look at that, will ya." She pointed to a rat running down the gutter. "Bloody filthy pigsty, ain't it? Just 'ope the whole bloody Yucatan ain't like this." She walked so fast I could barely keep up.

"Where are you going?" I asked.

"To the bus depot," she said.

"No, I mean to what city?"

She stopped and turned and stared at me with an eyebrow raised punishingly. "To Palenque, mate, to Palenque. And what about you?"

"Well, to Palenque too, I guess."

"Well, good." She turned and marched on. "That is if we can get a bloody bus out of this ruddy town."

We walked a couple of blocks and stopped on the corner. Yvette looked around, sensing the city with some weird instinct. She turned in every direction, looking here, looking there. "Okay, this way," she said, and accelerated down the street.

We hurried behind her to the next corner, turning left, then right at another corner, and damned if there in front of us wasn't some sort of a bus station. A sick little bus station, yes. Not second class, or third class, or peasant class—it was last class…or worse. Nash immediately shouted, "No, no, no, no!"

Yvette's face shined in delight. She had done it. Had negotiated the evil streets of Villahermosa and found the back door out. She marched into the station and pushed her way to the ticket seller—a card table in the corner of the room. She bought a ticket to Palenque, threw her pack on the floor, and sat on it.

Stef said, "I'm getting a ticket. What about you, Alex?"

"So am I," I said. "Come on, Nash, get a ticket. What else can we do?"

Nash was becoming very French. He was stubborn like a starving cat that refused to eat. He kept looking around the bus station, eyes rolling.

It was now almost daylight. The sky outside was pale blue. I didn't want to see Villahermosa in the day. We had been on the bus for almost a full day and were about to do it again.

Stef and I bought a ticket to Palenque. So did Nash…finally. Within thirty minutes, Stef and Nash and Yvette and I were sneaking out of Villahermosa—just in time.

I sat next to Yvette. She leaned against the raw wooden seat, pulled a bandana off her head, and let her brown hair hang loose. She was calmer now; I guess being free of Villahermosa helped.

She told me she was from Sydney, where she used to be a medical secretary. One day she decided to travel with a friend. Her friend stopped after two months and returned to Sydney. Yvette continued. That was twenty months ago. She had traveled through twelve countries. Except for transportation, she spent a dollar or two a day and at that rate had enough money to last another two years.

"I'm 'eading down to Central America," she said. "Guatemala and then El Salvador and Nicaragua and Costa Rica and Panama. And then into South America."

"There's a revolution going on in Nicaragua," I said.

"That's their business. I have no mind for that. All I want is to go through their country. You know there's a bloody revolution going on right here in Mexico. You just can't see it because it's not out in the open. But it's here. We could catch a bullet in the head any minute, especially on one of these ruddy buses. Sitting targets, we are. This whole country's a time bomb and suddenly, one day, poof, the whole bloody thing is going up in smoke."

The sun was now up. The Yucatan looked today as it did yesterday. The heat burned in through the window as if through a magnifying glass. I opened it to let air in. Across the aisle, Nash sat next to Stef. They talked as Stef looked out the window. After an hour or so we came to a fork in the road. Most of the people got off the bus, a few got on. We continued down two ruts carved through the jungle.

Nash took advantage of the extra space on the bus and walked around. Stef sat on the seat, legs stretched out, back propped against the side of the bus. Nash continued to walk up and down the aisle until the bus driver told him to sit down. Nash, of course, just swore at him in French and kept walking. I was no longer tired. My body had cycled completely through that and now was ready for a new day. I guess I had tricked it. Ha, ha!

The bus left the coastal road and cut into the Yucatan on one of the few trails inward. We traveled for a short while. Around eleven that morning, we arrived in Palenque. A small, simple village with nice white houses. This was the modern city of Palenque. The city of Palenque once inhabited by the Maya centuries ago was a mile or so into the jungle. We had arrived in the land of the people who once ruled across the Yucatan and most of Central America.

We went to the nearest restaurant and had eggs and beans and rice and had a tall glass of orange juice. After breakfast, we walked through the village and checked the price of a hotel room (too expensive).

We found a patch of clean grass on the edge of the village and set up our tents and strung our hammocks. I lay on the grass and looked at the plants and vines and flowers that dangled in the trees high above me. Everyone was lazy. We tried to sleep, but the tropical heat rejected our attempt. We talked about what to do. Yvette said we should go to the ruins before sunset.

Down a small path through the middle of the tropical forest teaming with birds and flowers and insects. The forest opened into a stretch of low green foliage and then, off in the distance, the statue-like temples of Palenque rose high.

As soon as I set foot on the grounds, I could tell it was a place of mystery—quiet and peaceful like the inside of an old cathedral. The grass and the plants and the flowers were rich with color. The green jungle was so dark it looked black. Old Mayan temples—

big stone structures—pushed through the jungle top toward the cerulean sky.

We were the only people in the vast courtyard of Palenque, shaped on all sides by stately temples—just the four of us, alone, not another soul, as though we were the first people to set foot in Palenque since the Maya left. I climbed a set of stairs that took me to the apex of the temple. There, I thought about the Maya, the creators of everything in Palenque.

I touched the stone slabs of the wall, rubbing my hand against its smooth surface as the ancient Maya must have done centuries ago. Leaning against the altar where holy rituals had been performed by the Mayan priests, sitting cross-legged on the top of the temple, I closed my eyes and thought about the Maya. I knew that they were a people driven to perfection, that they had a language so sophisticated much of it still remains obscure to us. A people with a calendar that repeated itself once every fifty-two years. Creators of everything at Palenque, all built without use of the wheel or metal tools, though they had knowledge of those. I wanted to learn everything about the Maya, to sit and talk to their priests, to find out what they knew.

I realized that the Maya had come to this place not by chance but for a reason. I felt energy rush through my body like bolts of harmless lightning. The energy was the answer—this I realized on top of the temple.

The Maya could use the energy. They could take its strength and its power and with it they could control their world. I knew this was the pure energy Miles spoke about, but I feared I may never understand it because my mind was permanently wired to the electric morphine of computers and gadgets. I had believed those gadgets would solve my problems. That they would provide the answers to the vast questions that burned inside me. I had believed those grand and deceptive creations of mankind would provide the answers to my questions. Oh, how I had been tricked into trusting the electric energy—that white-hot energy.

I don't know how long I stayed on top of the temple, an hour or two perhaps. The Mayan energy continued to pulse through me. In and out and around. Up into the cosmos and down again. As I thought about this, I discovered that the ancient Maya were still in Palenque. They had never left—they had merely evolved.

I couldn't reach them because my primitive brain didn't know how to. I was like a dog that understands a few words but not a whole sentence. I was listening, trying hard to hear. I realized that the secrets of the past, the secrets of everything in the past, were not gone. They were just hidden from me. If I wanted to find the secrets, it would require great patience and great persistence, and even disappointment. But these temples were the link between the past and the present. A conduit for the transfer of knowledge through time. The Maya had left all of this so we could reach them.

Could I reach the ancient Maya? I thought about the purity of that question. I discovered that time is not a physical thing—it exists all at once. Our rigid arrogant Western minds refuse to think this way. If I say: because I can't fly, does it mean no creature can fly. Because I exist in the present, then everything must exist in the present. The realization was simple, and it opened a million possibilities. It made the universe something more than a mere set of equations laid out by mankind's smartest minds. In our world, it would take more than a lifetime to get to the nearest star in conventional ways. But that's only if we did it in the present. If we went around time, distance is nothing but a neuronal creation that has no meaning. All of the universe is at our fingertips. But if we keep time linear, we're stuck with its linear implications.

I heard Stef calling. "Alex, come on. We're leaving. It's getting dark."

I looked out and saw that the sun was gone; Palenque was smothered in shadows. I climbed down the steps of the temple to where Stef and Nash and Yvette were waiting.

Stef asked if I liked Palenque.

I didn't know how to explain it, so I said it was good…very, very, good. I said was I was coming back tomorrow to spend the night on top of the temple. Nash looked at me as if I were crazy.

CHAPTER TWO

July 11, 1980 – Day 40

The next day was a wonderful one. We found a stream in the jungle with clear water that collected from a small waterfall into a pool about ten feet deep. We bathed and swam in the pool for most of the afternoon.

Up above were a thousand birds, talking and yakking in a noisy jamboree of voices. Spider monkeys watched with wide-open curious eyes. Nash found a vine and cut it loose at the bottom and we took turns swinging over the jungle pool, splashing into the water. Nash then tried to climb a tree, but halfway up he fell off onto his French head and decided it was all a stupid idea. Yvette climbed the tree, zipping up its trunk like a nimble monkey. She sat on one of its branches and yelped and jumped into the pool in a perfect swan dive. We applauded and the monkeys jumped up and down, causing the birds to scatter through the thicket of branches above us.

We went back to the camp feeling clean and fresh and later went into the town of Palenque and had dinner and drank ice-cold Tecate beer. Nash complained about the waiter, a child of twelve

or thirteen, the son of a poor Mexican couple who owned the restaurant. He was very inefficient, Nash grumbled. He informed us
that this boy would *never* get a job in a Paris café!

On the way to the camp, Yvette came up to me and said, "I'd
like to go to the temple with you tonight, Alex. I know Palenque
means a lot to you, I can tell. It's the same for me. Would it be a
problem if I came along?"

At first I didn't know what to say because I didn't know how
I felt about this. But before I could say anything, Yvette said, "I
don't want to go there alone, it might be dangerous. But I have to
go to Palenque tonight. I can't leave here without being up on the
temple as the Maya once were."

Then I knew it was right. I looked at Yvette. I saw the sincerity in her quiet but true eyes. "Sure, we'll go together. We'll go to
Palenque tonight. What d'ya say?"

"I say yay-es!" Yvette's face lit with joy.

Stef and Nash swung lazily in their hammocks. Yvette and I
filled our canteens with water. We took fruit and a blanket and as
the sun was beginning to set we started into the jungle. By the time
we made it to Palenque, a close darkness spread out across the
central courtyard. The lone Mexican groundkeeper had long since
gathered his things and left for the night. We climbed to the top of
the tallest temple; the jungle spread forth in steamy blackness in
every direction.

The moon—on its ascent into the sky to the left of us—shed
streaks of silver glitter across the top of the jungle and the stars
began to flicker as the sky glowed open and vast.

"This is the doorway to the universe, you know that don't

you, Alex?" Yvette said.

I looked at the sky. It was black as pitch, but it had life all through it. We stared at the flickering calcine cells that make up the universe.

"What do you think about the Maya, the people who built all this?" Yvette asked. "I think they're still all around us. We're up on the very top of their sacred temple. What will they think? What will they do?"

"They want us to be here," I said. "That's why the temple is here. That's why they built it out of solid stone so it will last ten thousand, maybe twenty thousand years, maybe longer. We don't build things like that because we have no faith in our future. The Maya knew that without the future there is no present, and without the present there is only the past. And the past by itself is worthless."

We watched the jungle shift and sway in its moony glow. Insects sang their crisp songs and a howler monkey called out its lone shrill cry. The breeze of the night air was sweet and heavy upon us. Again, I felt the energy as I had the previous day.

Yvette was right about this being the window to the universe. Children we were, at the doorstep of existence. And like all children, we had few expectations. We were once again innocent and ready for whatever would come, and I knew that whatever it was, it would be good, because in innocence everything is good.

"There is powerful energy up here," I said. "I felt it the first time I was here, and now I feel it again today."

A soft breeze, almost cool at times, blew across the top of the jungle. The moon was a slice of soft light aimed down onto our stage. The stars and the sky and the whole universe were our audience. We were there for them and they were there for us, just as in any good theater. We rested against the carved stone altar and closed our eyes.

I held Yvette's hand and thought about the jungle and the universe. Then my mind was wiped clean of all of its distracting thoughts. All awareness vanished except for the spiritual presence of the Maya and Yvette next to me. My mind was drenched in a voided emptiness. I made no effort to direct its thoughts as I slipped deeper and deeper into a peaceful calm until all physical sensation stopped and for the first time ever I was free in the universe. I was alert and aware and exalted, soaring free. I had no ties to the Earth. I saw another life form—a full dimension beyond our own.

I met a Mayan chief named Chatka. He spoke in perfect clear words, though some of what he said was like a riddle that I couldn't understand. He said he had been born in Palenque in our year of 637 AD, and that in 663 AD he was transformed to the second phase of his life, and since then he'd been back to Palenque several times. He told me that I had come to what the ancient Maya called Pachota, which means goodwill. In Pachota, all things are possible. He said the Earth is a good place and the Maya will never abandon it unless it becomes uninhabitable for life.

Chatka talked of many things I didn't understand. I told him so. He said they would become clear to me, like a dream that is obscure at first, then makes sense later. He said the answer to everything is available; nothing is impossible. It's merely that we don't understand it. Just then, Miles, the poet from San Miguel, appeared. I saw his burly face and straight black hair and deep brown eyes and the vague outline of his tattered poncho. Chatka stopped talking and Miles spoke, telling me things as if we were sitting in the sunny café across from the zocalo. He said he knew we'd meet again in Palenque. Miles said Andy and Chloe were fine, and that Andy was close to finishing his book and was going to take it easy for the rest of the summer before starting to rewrite it.

Miles told me everything about Miguel, and then he said he had a message to convey but he never said what it was. After all was said, Chatka and Miles left and again I was in the black void. I opened my eyes and saw the jungle with the moon high over the sky. Yvette sat next to me. Her eyes were closed, though she appeared not to be asleep. It was two thirty according to my watch. I had been gone for over five hours. I felt rested and wonderful. Yvette opened her eyes and looked at me. We made love on the altar on top of the temple under the moon, under the whole universe. It seemed so long since I had held someone.

Later we ate fruit and drank water and made love again on a patch of grass below the temple. The sun came up and Yvette walked naked around Palenque in the green-gray morning mist. I climbed back up to the top of the temple and sat and watched her curious wanderings. In the pocket of my shirt I found a piece of paper with a poem that said:

nothing hurts like
missing
nothing fills me

up so empty

as missing

just so full of

missing

Immediately I knew this was Miles's message—though not from him but from Maureen through Miles. Every inch of me felt sad and all I could do was cry. Yvette got dressed and came up and sat next to me. Sun broke across the jungle and the leaves and the grass sparked with morning dew and it was already as hot as midday in Mississippi.

We left Palenque and walked through the deep green forest that appeared more spectacular and more beautiful than ever. Arriving at the jungle waterhole, we bathed and swam in the heat of the early sun that burrowed down through the steamy morning air, making the world misty and queer.

We started into the jungle down a winding narrow footpath. As we turned the corner, we came face to face with a huge wild boar, tall as my waist with glassy eyes and two long sharp tusks. It so startled Yvette that she screamed, causing the boar to stand frozen in place before us. We stood motionless, trapped by the jungle on all sides with nowhere to retreat to except back down the path. I reached frantically for the knife I kept strapped on my belt, but my hand was clumsy and nervous. Nor did I know what I would do against the massive animal that challenged us.

Yvette was scared—it was the first time I'd seen her like that. The boar pulled its head to the ground like a bull. It snorted. Its tusks aimed firmly at us, not six feet away.

"We have to give it room or it will feel trapped," I said softly. "It means business."

Yvette was frozen in place. I stepped back and pulled her behind me. "Real slow," I said. "Back up."

The boar snorted again, stared, waited, and then pulled its head up and was quickly off.

Yvette was pale—her whole frame trembled. She said, "I don't like those bloody things, Alex. They scare the hell out of me.

"They scare the hell out of me, too."

"What would we do if it came at us?"

"I don't know. Try to get out of the way, I guess. That thing weighed a good eight hundred pounds, more probably. We'd be no match for it."

In the afternoon Stef returned to the ruins to photograph. Nash wandered about in the jungle. We were now ready to leave Palenque—each of us had gotten what we had come for.

We made dinner. Nash said a train ran by Palenque every day at midnight. After dinner we packed up and around ten o'clock set off for the station. We staggered through the blistering night heat until we reached a small town. A dark sleepy-looking place. We followed Nash down a gloomy road, not sure where he was going. Nash gets lost a lot. (No wonder he got screwed up in Nashville. None of those instincts of Yvette's). "Right behind you, Nash," I said. We turned a corner and there before us was a set of tracks, a shack, and people.

ʎ

We set our packs against the shack, a small feeble building made of wood from old orange crates. Everything about the station seems surreal. Open windows, no glass, no screen, bare yellow electric bulb outside, bare yellow electric bulb inside, lots of people, lots of packs piled everywhere. More people come in from the jungle. Jungle rats getting high on Palenque. I look around. I hear five, six, seven—no, maybe eight languages. We go inside. More people. Gringos, Mexicans. People sit at a table playing cards. Two young Mexican boys in National Guard uniforms, kids with carbines and green fatigues. One of them leans against the wall, sleepy, eyes closing. The other plays cards at the table, gun across his lap.

"Four tickets," Nash says to the woman at the window.

"No tickets, pay on train. Want gum?" She holds up gum. "Un peso…want Coca-Cola?" She holds up Coca-Cola. "Want beers?" Holds up beer.

Nash buys four beers. He hands one to each of us. The room is unforgivingly hot—smoky and humid. Quavering shadows spread out across the room from the one sad and lonely bulb. Faces looked funny, dripped in shadows. Beer tastes good. Sweat runs off my face. My hair sticks to my forehead and neck. Stef gets a cigarette from the old lady and shares it with Nash as they watch the card players. Everyone drinks beer. The young army boy drinks beer. Yvette and I go outside—a dark muddy night, no moon, no stars. Thick air.

More people arrive. A German man with a French woman asks what time the train will arrive.

"Midnight," I say.

"Have you been to Palenque?" Yvette asks.

"Yes, and out into the jungle, too," says the French woman.

They go inside.

Insects dance around the light bulb—a death dance in the night. The bare bulb glows yellow against the black night.

Yvette says she will remember Palenque forever. "The Yucatan is full of magic, isn't it?"

I go inside for a minute and come back out.

"What's going on?" Yvette asks.

"People drinking beer and playing cards."

We go in and watch the card players.

The army boy tries to talk to me in English; he stares at Yvette the whole while.

Down the tracks, a train lurches toward the station. I look at my watch—eleven o'clock. It's not our train, the army boy tells us. It's the milk train for the peasants. We want El Rapido, he tells us. That will come at midnight. Have to see that to believe it, I think. The train arrives, people get on. The train leaves and we're back inside.

I sip beer. We're going to Merida, almost three hundred miles into the Yucatan, could take six hours, could take sixty. I look at Yvette. She looks good in the sad, crazy, yellow light—funny sort of person, real different, always sexy even in the sweltering jungle. Stef watches the card players and drinks beer. Nash sits at the table and plays cards. He waves to the woman and she brings him a beer. Nash looks real cool, real suave, cards in his hand, cigarette dangling from his mouth, talking to the cards in French, telling them what to do. He bets two cigarettes. Someone raises two. Nash calls and wins. "Ho, boy! Ho, boy! Ho, boy!" He picks up the cigarettes. They deal again. Lots more people come in. Don't know from where. Never saw anyone in the jungle.

Eleven forty-five. A train comes down the track. Can't be ours, but it is. Fifteen minutes early! Everyone is up. Stef yells to me, "Get my pack, Alex."

I pick up the packs and we jam toward the train. Everyone gets on—don't want to be left behind. The station is empty now. With a jolt we're off, leaving Palenque, leaving the ruins. I look out the door and watch the shack shrink behind us. Yvette watches too.

CHAPTER THREE

July 12, 1980 – Day 41

Wow, El Rapido was painfully crowded!

"This is a hell of a train, Alex," Yvette beamed.

Now I believed all trains in Mexico were crowded, and a little dirty, and slow. Even the ones called Rapido. I looked into one of the cars. Everyone was settled in for the night, ready for a long trip through the Yucatan. It was cooler out between the cars, so we stayed there for a while sitting on our packs. A man came by selling cold drinks. He walked through the car. "Cervezas!"

The train rolled on.

"I'm sleeping right here," Nash said. "And I don't give a damn what anyone says. I'm not sitting in that rotten car."

I leaned against the hard steel frame of the train. Yvette sat next to me. Nash and Stef sat across from us. Night air washed through the open doorway. It felt good to be on this miserable train riding through a lost world, all of us just as lost as that world.

Yvette put her hand on my cheek. "But it's a good train, ain't it, mate?"

"Yeah, mate," I said, "it's a good train. A damn good train."

The night became more and more still. Nash wandered restlessly through the train. He returned and told us to quick grab our packs. We followed him until we arrived at the very end of the train where Nash led us onto a platform just big enough for the four of us.

Stef beamed. "This is tremendous! Look at it. Look at the jungle out there. Look at the whole damn world. Christ, look at the sky!"

We sat on the platform. Nash pulled out a joint. He lit it and passed it around. We took precious drags till our lungs burned. The train rocked steady and slow as the jungle fell behind us. The marijuana made us as quiet as the night that surrounded us. No one said much except for Nash, who talked incessantly, saying things like he was glad to be at the back of the train because he didn't trust the Mexican engineers, and if the train crashed, we would be the last ones to know it. He wondered how many flat wheels the train would get. He wanted to climb on top of the train and see how many spare wheels they had.

There was a wrought-iron railing around the platform that kept us from falling into the Yucatan. I lay down and in no time I was fast asleep. I slept straight through the night, and when I awoke it was early morning. I could see steam rising from the jungle. Stef and Nash were gone. Yvette was sitting up watching the Yucatan. I felt wonderful. I loved the feeling of being connected to some endless train that roared on forever.

Yvette said she slept well and asked how I slept.

"Like a baby," I replied.

"Stef didn't sleep much," she said.

I saw the vendor inside the car—this time selling coffee. I bought a cup for Yvette and myself. We drank the rich dark liquid in the morning sun. Soon we would be in Merida on the tip of the Yucatan.

Stef came out onto the platform. He said he had spent the night in the cars stealing images of the poor Mexican train people. "I got some great shots," he said. "And even the old conductor who had nothing else to do helped out just to break the boredom of his job. We went from car to car all night. He was great."

"Where's Nash?" I asked.

Stef shrugged. "He's around somewhere…but they almost threw him off the train at the last stop because he started arguing with the vendor over the price of coffee. Nash started swearing and saying, 'Fock you, Fock you.' The conductor got pissed and tried to get him off the train until I came and talked him out of it. Nash is fuming now. He's sitting between the cars mad at everything."

"Well, I hope he snaps out of it before we leave this train," Yvette said.

Stef said he would. "That's just the way he is."

We had become an odd little family, traipsing through the Yucatan together. We pulled together when we needed to. We could be alone when we needed to. We could go off and sulk knowing that sooner or later someone would come by and help us out of our sulk. A train in the jungle can be a lonely experience, but together we shared each other's delights and each other's miseries.

We sat happily on the platform knowing soon we'd be in

Merida. Nash eventually joined us. He was no longer mad at the world; he was anxious to get to Merida.

It's a pretty city," Nash said. "A French woman inside the train told me."

"What day is it?" Stef asked.

Saturday or Sunday, no one quite knew.

"It's the Thirteenth," I said.

"Of July?" Nash, who had been traveling for months, asked.

"Oh, yes, of July. *That* much I'm sure of," Yvette said.

"So it's either Saturday or Sunday, the Thirteenth of July."

"I think that's right," Nash said.

At ten in the morning, we arrived in Merida. We took our things and walked out into the streets of the capital of the Yucatan. Merida is a pretty city, part Spanish and part Caribbean. We had breakfast at a café. We would get a hotel room for the night—the first in almost a week. Nash and Yvette searched for a room while Stef and I waited at the café.

Stef slumped in the chair and looked up toward the sky. He asked about Yvette.

"She's a special sort of person," I said. "Lots of spunk. I like that."

"Are you in love with her?"

"Well, no," I replied, "I've only known her for a few days."

Stef nodded. "Uh-huh, just wondering. What do you think of Merida?"

"It looks good, from here anyway. It's pretty." After a long while, I said, "You know, Stef, we've been gone for nearly six weeks now."

"Could be six months," Stef said.

"Feels like six months and yet it seems like nothing at all. I don't know, Stef, I may never go back. I may just keep going on down through Central America and then to South America…and after that, I don't know. That's where Yvette's headed…South America. My money's holding out pretty well."

Stef leaned back in the chair. I could tell he was still thinking about San Miguel. After a while he confessed as much. "I could go work with Andy, or just go there and do my own thing. There's not much for me in Baltimore except a small flat up on Bolton Hill," Stef said. His voice betrayed confident uncertainty.

Nash and Yvette returned with the good news that they had found a place to stay for the night. One great big room with four beds in a beautiful old hotel with a wonderful swimming pool, all for only two dollars and fifty cents each. Oh, yes, and a big clean shower. Together they were a grand team, Nash and Yvette. If there was a bargain to be had, they'd find it—and Mexico was full of bargains.

We stayed in Merida for several days. Life was easy, living in our comfortable room, eating and drinking in the cafés. But soon we had outgrown Merida and again had the craving for the road. Early one morning we packed up and were on a bus heading east through the low tropical forest to the Caribbean coast.

It was a simple ride of two hours or so from Merida to Cancun. But Cancun, with its big hotels and rich tourists in white shorts and white polo shirts, was not for us. And, for that matter, they didn't seem to like the disturbing appearance of riffraff like us walking through the streets of their paunchy resort.

I talked to a Mexican cab driver named Pablo. He said to go up the coast a short way and there we'd find a ferry that would get us to an island called Isla de Mujeres—Isla Mujeres as it's known. After the desert and the jungles and the buses and the trains, a small tropical island made great sense. We took Pablo's advice and started for the ferry dock.

If you grew up in Chicago near Lake Michigan and then lived in Baltimore near the Chesapeake Bay, your mind had no capacity to imagine anything as pure and wonderful as the Caribbean—blue and turquoise and emerald green. Again, I was a child as I hung over the side of the boat and looked down into the pristine world below. I wanted to be a fish—to swim and skip through the water—diving and jumping and circling and turning in the coral canyons beneath us. I looked at the sky, all blue and warm. The spray that came off the front of the boat from the ocean cooled my face. I was happy to be with Stef and Yvette and Nash. So happy to be so happy.

On the ferry, a Mexican boy came by and collected our fares. We were now out of sight of the shoreline. In the distance I could see Isla Mujeres. Our boat was filled to the gills with people. These, however, were the more fortunate of Mexico's poor. *Better to be a peasant on a tropical island than in a tin can of Mexico City or Vera Cruz*, I thought. I saw life in these people.

At Isla Mujeres we took our packs and started down a street toward the center of the island, passing adobe buildings painted blue and white and turquoise as clean as the Caribbean itself. We saw shops and restaurants and barefoot islanders who wore straw hats as they rode through the streets on bikes and scooters. People stopped and watched us and every now and then one would wave or call out, "Hola!"

The island was small—a half dozen simple hotels and a couple of modestly priced places. I asked an islander where we could stay for the night. He told us about a place on the tip of the island called La Hamaca. He said it was cheap if you had your own hammock to string up. As we walked to La Hamaca, Yvette bubbled with joy. "This is our little island," she said, dancing sideways and backwards and forwards. "It's all ours. Yours and yours and yours and mine. All ours. Isn't it great? Don't you love it?"

I did. We all did. Even Nash liked Isla Mujeres. This is where we had been headed all along, from the desert into the mountains and through the jungle. Our trek had led us to this immaculate little island—a pot of gold, a fountain of youth in the crystal waters of the Caribbean.

La Hamaca was owned by an American named Michael, who'd lived most of his life on Isla Mujeres. We strung our hammocks under a big cabana made of thatched palm leaves and large open windows that permitted the sea breeze to come and go as it wished. We lay in our hammocks, being lazy and feeling good and very, very happy.

CHAPTER FOUR

July 16, 1980 – Day 45

On Isla Mujeres, time passed unnoticed. The days came and went like the tides, and each day became more special than the one before. I discovered a whole new part of life. Things that once were important became meaningless, and little things took on importance. Each day was an adventure in life. We got up early and drank delicious coffee and ate sweet bread for breakfast. Mornings, we were swimming in the calm waters off the north end of the island. We toasted in the sun until noon and then had a good meal of red snapper, or conch, or shrimp, and drank beer with our lunch.

By three o'clock we were on the south end at Garafon Beach where the reef connects with the island. We swam through the water and dove to the bottom next to the coral wall through schools of fish that parted like silky curtains as we passed through.

We did this day after day until time became an abstract thing. In one way or another, everything we did drew meaning from everything else we did. Life was interwoven and connected and I began to treasure the present more than any fantasy of the future.

Of course, we were not the only travelers staying at La

Hamaca. There were a few others like us who carelessly ended up on the island. But Michael, the owner, took a liking to us, and it was hard not to find good things to like about him. He was a handsome man with skin darkened by the sun and sandy hair that hung loose, never combed, never messy. He had strong cheekbones and a good jaw and soft hazel eyes. He always wore jeans or khaki shorts and a T-shirt, and he liked to laugh and kid and joke. Nothing seemed to bother or worry him.

He told us he had come to Mexico from the States with his mother when he was sixteen—first living in the Yucatan, then when he was twenty he came to Mujeres. He ran a shop on the island, fished for a while, and then bought the La Hamaca. Michael's Spanish was almost flawless. He had a Mexican lover named Concepcion who went by the name Coca. She would come to La Hamaca in the evening with Francisco, her eight-year-old son from a previous marriage.

One evening Michael grilled fresh snapper and the four of us and he and Coca and Francisco had a feast of fish with rice and sliced avocado and lots of cold beer and tequila with lime.

I thought Michael was the luckiest man in the world to have this place out on a spectacular island, to be content in a world of which he was so much a part. You could tell his love for Coca was deep. He seemed to be as happy with her as he was with everything about his life—with her simplicity and her beautiful Mexican features. But more than anything it was the relationship between Michael and little Francisco that seemed to hold special sway with Michael. And for Francisco, Michael was part man, part perfection. Nothing in this world existed that Michael didn't know or couldn't do. Being a child, Francisco was a sponge for knowledge and information. "El Doctor," is what Michael called Francisco, or sometimes "El Doctorito," the "little doctor," the peasant child from the lost island of Isla Mujeres who would grow up confident and smart under Michael's careful direction. He would study at a good university and someday he would be a great surgeon or a great specialist. When Michael told Francisco this, you could almost see the boy's pride burst from his body.

After dinner, we all took a walk along the beach. The moon was nearly full; it reflected on the water like on fine crystal. A warm breeze blew across the island. Francisco ran ahead, picking up shells that he brought back for Michael's inspection. Michael rubbed the shells with his thumb and said, "Ah, this is a fine one, Francisco." Francisco deposited the piece in his pocket and searched again for another treasure. Coca walked next to Michael, patient and content. I thought for sure that I had landed in paradise. As we walked along, Yvette quietly touched my hand and held it softly. In that one simple moment, I sensed the beginning of something new.

The days flew by. Eventually we became like the islanders. We had little need for the rest of the world with its insanity and politics, its assassinations and nuclear arsenals. Life for us was basic and satisfying. When I read a newspaper brought in from the mainland, when I read about the lunacy of the leaders in Washington and Moscow and London, I couldn't help but wonder how it was that civilization had made such a wrong turn. How could we be so far off course and not know it? When people go crazy, they are sometimes unaware of it because they have lost all sense of reality. So too with nations? Can a whole nation lose its mind? The whole world—the entire planet? As I sat on the virgin beaches of Isla Mujeres, I thought about these things. As I watched the people on the island go about their daily business, I realized they didn't care at all about the petty differences that exist between Washington and Moscow and London. I thought about those people, the powers of the world, and I wondered why they believed they had the right to toy with life on this planet, to disrupt the lives of people who were living a good, pure, and decent existence—bothering nobody.

Weeks passed. I gave less thought to the world's insanity and more to swimming in the crystalline waters off Garafon. We used an old homemade speargun that Michael gave us, fashioned out of a hollow steel cylinder with a thick rubber strap across the back that sent a metal spear tearing through the water as good as any expensive version.

We swam through the fish-bloated water carrying the speargun. With a touch of luck, we had dinner for the night: red snapper or flounder or some other choice meal delivered up from the sea.

It all went well until the blood from the impaled fish brought sharks into our little cove. When that happened, we were out of the water quickly, especially when the hammerheads or bull sharks came in.

Each day we got better at fishing and almost always came back with a good catch. We took turns using the speargun. We could all bring in food, and never caught more than we could eat.

We got to know the islanders, especially the divers who collected shells from the deep parts of the reef. Diving for conch was dangerous. All the divers were strong lean men with bodies tight as steel cables. They could swim through the roughest waters, frequently diving past barracudas to get at the shells on the bottom. In the water, the divers were fearless men who faced the unknown surprises of the reef every day. But on land they were happy and seemed not to have a care in the world. I noticed they all had good clear eyes as though they could sense trouble long before it happened.

Often, a diver named Sal came with us to Garafon. We swam with him out to the reef. He glided through the water like a porpoise, effortless, circling down into the water for up to a minute without coming up for air. Sal taught us about the reef. How to search for the langostas, the lobsters, that hide on the ocean floor. He told us what was poisonous, what was safe, what to avoid, and what was good to eat. Perhaps most importantly, he told us what to do if a shark or a barracuda came too close. Everything we learned from Sal was important and made sense in some way.

CHAPTER FIVE

August 8, 1980 – Day 67

One morning instead of going to swim, I went to the café and wrote a letter to my parents, and a long letter to Maureen, telling her everything that had happened to me and Stef. I told her about our neat little island and my new life and all the changes I felt and all the good things I was experiencing. I told her about Nash and Michael and La Hamaca—everyone except Yvette. Whatever needed to be said about her, I wasn't ready to do it because I didn't yet know how to accept that part of my new life. So I hid it from Maureen—and cautiously from myself as well.

Late in the morning, Sal walked past the café. Odd to find him in town and not out fishing during the day. He sat at the table and ordered a drink.

"Storm coming," he said, "can't dive…sea too rough."

The day looked fine to me, shiny as the string of shells around Sal's neck.

Shortly after that, Yvette and Nash and Stef turned up. They confirmed what Sal had said about a storm.

By late in the afternoon, the sky was full of thick swirling clouds and by three o'clock rain was coming in squalls and already you could tell it was just a small part of a big storm.

We went back to La Hamaca and played cards and watched the water run off the grass roof onto the side of the building where it collected in little streams and then into bigger streams and finally into ankle-deep torrents that gushed into the streets.

Michael came by and sat with us. "Great big storm…a hurricane…it's called Allen. It's already between Jamaica and Cuba, just east of us. I've been following it for a while. Didn't look like it would be much of anything. Then suddenly it grew into a real whopper."

"Is it coming here?" Yvette asked.

"No one knows for sure. Could go north across Cuba and up into Florida. If it does, we'll mostly be spared. Or it might come west. If so…well. It's growing stronger real fast. Might make it up to a category five, they say. Ton of rain, lots of wind…a hundred and eighty miles an hour or so."

"When will we know which way it's going?" Stef asked.

"By about seven tonight probably," Michael said.

"If the hurricane came here, what would it do to the island?" I asked.

Michael shook his head. "We've never had a direct hit by a hurricane this size in the twenty years I've been here. Storms, but never like this. I don't know what will happen. This is a small island. Look over your left shoulder and you can see one side of the island…to the right, the other side. I don't know how much Mujeres could take."

The rain drummed angrily on the roof. The sky was nearly

black; the inside of the cabana was dark. As Michael spoke, the lights flickered and went dead; he retrieved a kerosene lamp. In the bleak light from the lamp, he said, "Most of the island is getting ready for the worst."

"We should leave, don't you think? Everyone should leave the island," Nash implored.

"The ferry stopped running three hours ago," Michael replied. "The waves are growing fast. Pretty soon there'll be fifteen to twenty foot swells…there's no way off now."

"Well, they'll evacuate us then," Nash said. "Someone will come in with helicopters or something and clear the island. They can't let this happen. We're still people, aren't we? Don't we matter to anyone? Doesn't life mean anything down here? Well? Doesn't it?" Nash looked at us for an answer. We knew the answer just as he did. He stared at us, each, one at a time, then slumped into his hammock, eyes rolled back in his head. A look of anger and disgust came over him.

By six o'clock, the rain was coming in sheets and the sky was black and the wind had teeth. We waited—the four of us, and Coca and Francisco—for Michael's report on the storm. But he could learn nothing by six o'clock as the storm was still out at sea with all its rage. At seven o'clock, we listened as the verdict scratched out of Michael's marine radio. We heard it together. "It's coming for Mujeres," Michael uttered.

There was a moment of great silence as we sat motionless. Nash wheezed and said, "What do we do?"

Michael said, "There's a shelter on the back of the island. It should be safe there. All of you, and you too," talking to Coca, "and you my little amigo, I want all of you to go to the shelter for safety." Then he looked back at Francisco. "You take care of mama…entiendes?"

"What about you?" Yvette asked.

"I'm staying here," Michael said. "This is everything I own in the whole world." He looked about La Hamaca. "She's a lot tougher than she looks; she's built pretty well. We could lose some of the roof, I suppose, but the rest will make it. That's my bet."

Coca wanted to stay with Michael at La Hamaca; after all, he was all she had too. But that was out of the question. Michael's resolve was firm. We helped Michael nail plywood across the open windows of the building and gathered our things together.

All evening, an old dump truck came through the streets of Mujeres. A man with a megaphone called out to the islanders, telling them to leave their homes and go to the shelter on the high part of the island. People climbed onto the truck. It took them to the shelter and returned for more people. Some islanders refused to go, afraid of abandoning their huts and their goats and their chickens.

The men pleaded with everyone to leave, but when it was very late and when the hurricane was nearing, they gave up and left for the shelter.

We climbed onto the truck and rode through the dark empty streets of Mujeres as a deadly evil rain terrorized the island. The pastel shops and the houses and the cafés where I once saw hope were now full of gloom. It seemed like a long ride to the shelter— very long and very ugly and very somber.

The shelter was a big circular building made of cinder blocks and concrete. It looked secure, strong enough for most storms. Hundreds of islanders gathered inside. I saw people we knew. Sal, the diver, came over and talked briefly to us, but he couldn't say much because he was too drunk. His clear eyes were now moist and glassy. He walked across the shelter to the far wall and spread out a blanket and went to sleep. I wondered what that meant. Sal once told me he would never dive when he had been drinking because a shark can spot weakness, and a wounded animal has no chance against a shark. Seeing Sal in his present state made me realize that what we faced was not a shark. It was much bigger and much stronger. It would get its way, and we would have little to say about it.

I looked around. Yes, we were nothing but a school of fish drifting in the ocean. I could tell Stef and Nash and Yvette knew this also. There was something out in the darkness coming toward us, closer each minute. Was it wind and rain and thunder, just that and nothing more? Or was it…an end to something. The end is always a thing in the future, isn't it? Even the most morbid mind can't fully perceive its own end until it is right there, inevitable, about to happen. Until it has actually started. Could this be the start?

The rain beat viciously on the shelter. Outside, the tall palms and rubber trees were bent at the waist like old men. Rain tore across the land, not falling from the sky but swirling in petrifying sheaves over the island. The strength of the wind was so great I could almost feel it blowing through the concrete blocks of the shelter. I knew then that our shelter was nothing more than a grass hut. And the hurricane had yet to arrive.

Nine o'clock, the winds got stronger and louder. Stef stood by the door of the shelter talking to the Mexicans. He came back and said he was going into Mujeres with the Mexicans in a last attempt to save the ones still in town.

"This is crazy, Stef," I screamed. "What do you mean you're going into Mujeres. The hurricane is damn near here. Mujeres will be destroyed. There will be nothing left of that part of the island!"

"And there will be nothing left of this place either," Stef said, as he stuffed things into a canvas bag.

"Stef, listen to me! Are you nuts? You can't do this," I said.

The Mexicans yelled for Stef to hurry.

Nash said, "To go into Mujeres now is a death wish."

Yvette tried also. It was no use. Stef put on his rain poncho and wrapped himself around and around with surgical tape. The Mexicans at the door waved to hurry. Stef started for the truck.

I grabbed my poncho. "Then I'm going too," I said.

Yvette screamed and ran after me, "Then so am I," she said.

I held Yvette by the shoulders. "No!" I demanded. "You can't. You have to stay here."

Stef turned and said, "Alex, let's go." He looked at Yvette. "You must stay here with Nash. We'll both be back. Just wait here."

Nash held Yvette. Stef and I climbed onto the back of the truck under a canvas top stretched across a metal frame. Two Mexicans sat up front. We started out into a black night, into a black storm, into a black hell.

CHAPTER SIX

August 8, 1980 – Day 67

The truck hydroplaned across the road through currents of water. We held tight onto the frame of the truck as the wind cut into us at a hundred and twenty-five miles an hour. I felt an evilness in the hurricane that was so strong it smelled. Stef stared firmly out the back of the truck and turned and looked at me with the look of a crazed hyena.

We drove slowly through the dark village. The tears of the storm beat down on everything so that the roads were nothing more than a flowing junction between the two halves of the sea. The shops and restaurants were closed and the cafés where not long ago we had sat and drank beer and rum in the happy afternoons were now just black holes in the night.

As we rode through the street, the two Mexicans in the front of the truck called out with a megaphone, telling people to give up the darkness and come to the shelter. A man and a woman with a child ran from a hut—we pulled them onto the back of the truck. Soon two more people came out and climbed on. The wind was full now. It snapped palm trees at the trunk as though exploded by dynamite. The tops of trees—branches and coconuts, the works—

spun through the air like newspaper. I felt the truck lift off the ground with each gust, and with one quick gust, the canvas tarp that covered the back of the truck was ripped off and we were naked to the storm. The tarp spun up into the air, sucked into a funnel of wind.

In a doorway not far from us, a woman and child clung to the house as she called desperately. We tried to get near, but the water was too high. The truck lurched along, choking, until in a spasm it died in the road in a gush of water.

The woman screamed as water began to pour out the front door, pulling them into the street. Stef crawled to the edge of the truck. He tried to stand but the wind knocked him back. The water was coming out of the house in swells. The woman was losing her grip; the baby looked dead or unconscious. Stef dove off the truck into the water. He spun like a bottle. I saw him go under and come up and go down again, and then come up. As he passed the house, he reached for a lamp post and made a great leap and reached the woman and child.

The driver worked the engine, turning it over again and again until the battery was nearly dead. Each time the engine gasped and quit. In one last attempt, it fired off. The driver raced the engine, pumping gas into the wet guts of the motor. He jammed the truck into gear as we pulled Stef and the others on board.

We were almost at the end of Mujeres. The ocean gushed across the island. Huts that once were there were gone. Trees were nothing more than leafless spears. In the black, gray, brown night, I watched as we inched closer to La Hamaca. I couldn't imagine how anything could remain in all this. I felt my heart grind in my chest as we turned down the small alley that led to La Hamaca.

The little store on the corner was gone; an overturned car blocked the road. The truck squeezed around the car and up ahead I saw La Hamaca—all there except for the grass roof that had been sheared off.

The driver stopped the truck, afraid of stalling again. Stef pounded on the window at the back of the truck and ordered him to drive forward. The wind was vicious; the rain blinded us. As we approached La Hamaca, Stef told the driver to pull near one of the windows. We climbed onto the window ledge and went into the front room. It was black and cold inside, but I felt as though there was a good chance Michael was all right. We called for him, inching across the room, slowly, carefully, watching the loose pieces of ceiling that dangled above us. At times the whole place shook as the storm slammed it.

"I don't see him," Stef said.

"Well, then he must've left," I replied.

"But there's nowhere to go."

"Then he's here somewhere. He must be." I called out as we moved through La Hamaca.

We walked farther and still no sign of Michael. We were near the back of La Hamaca where Michael's personal living quarters were. That's where we'd find him, I figured, unable to hear us because of the lungs of the storm. We moved along slowly in knee-deep water that churned at our feet. Stef carried the light. I followed a few steps behind, feeling my way forward in the tattered glow of the flashlight.

Michael's room was empty except for the flooded water.

Nothing was out of place—still no sign of Michael. I looked around for a clue, anything to tell us where he'd gone. Stef opened the door to the back room Michael used for storage. Alone in the blackness, I felt my way to where Stef had vanished, bumping into chairs and other things as I went.

"Where are you, Stef?" I called. I got no answer, as if Stef had fallen into some deep black hole created by the hurricane. He had vanished just as Michael seemed to have. As I neared the door, I heard things being moved around in the storage room. I heard Stef's voice, talking to...to himself, I think. Or maybe to Michael. Michael must be in there.

"Stef, Stef!" I called. "Come here, give me some light. Where are you?"

As I said that, Stef appeared in front of me, wet and pale and ghostly looking.

"Where the hell's Michael?" I asked. "What the hell's going on, Stef. Give me some light."

"No, no, Alex," Stef said as he pushed me out of the room.

"What is it, Stef? It's Michael, isn't it? Michael's in there." I looked at Stef and saw his chalky face and lifeless eyes and then, right then, I knew what had happened.

"Oh, Christ," I said, "he's...Michael's.... Oh, Christ. Michael's in there?"

Stef nodded.

"He's hurt?"

Stef continued to lead me away from the door. "No, Alex...." Stef's voice cracked. He stopped talking and caught his breath, "No, Alex." He paused again, then finally said, "Michael's dead."

Stef swore and began to cry and through bursts of tears he said something about the roof caving in, pinning Michael under one of the beams.

"Oh, Jesus," I said. I felt my stomach turn inside out.

Stef screamed at the storm—this living thing of destruction that had descended on us. "You're not so tough. Do you hear! You're not so goddamn tough! You just wait, you won't get away with this! You'll never get away with this! You're not so goddamn tough! Do you hear me? Do you?"

I held Stef. When he had calmed down, we went into the room and lifted the beam that had stolen Michael's life. As we carried him out of La Hamaca, I could tell his spine had been broken. His back was limp like a rabbit with a busted neck. We laid him on the back of the truck and drove to the shelter in the cold empty night. Now, for the first time, I was no longer afraid of the storm. I no longer worried about its rain or its wind or its power. I realized that fear comes from intimidation, and I was no longer intimidated.

We stopped and picked up more people on the way back. In all, there were about a dozen of us in the back of the truck, plus Michael's puffy body, which we had covered with coats.

People packed into the doorway and watched as we drove up to the shelter. We filed in carrying Michael's body from the truck; people parted like wheat stalks as we passed.

The shelter was damp and dark and filled with that same evil smell of the hurricane. Clusters of islanders huddled in pockets around the shelter. Stef and I and the two Mexicans from the truck carried Michael's body to the back of the shelter where the town

officials were running things, doling out food and tortillas. Rodriguez, the mayor of Isla Mujeres, watched with empty eyes as we
laid Michael's body on planks of wood—one of many bodies that
would be set there before all was finished. Those of us who had
just returned from being out in the storm knew that, and I could
tell Rodriguez knew this too.

Coca pushed her way through the crowd and stood staring at
the body she knew was Michael's. Then she looked at me, waiting
for me to say, 'No, Coca, it's not Michael. He's fine back at La
Hamaca and everything's okay, don't worry.' Oh, how I wished I
could have said that. How I wished I could have changed reality,
altered it, corrected it. But powerless I was. Impotent to do anything but stand, beat up, half-drowned, words themselves stolen
from my mouth—and those unspoken words screamed out to Coca
of Michael's death. Coca grabbed her hair in tight knotted fists and
screamed her pain. Tears greater than all the storm itself flowed
down her face.

Nash clenched his teeth as he stared at the tarp that hid
Michael's body. Yvette stared, catatonically, covering her mouth.
Tears streamed down her cheeks. She slumped to the floor under
the weight of the moment and wept like a child. Dripping wet and
muddy, I sat next to Yvette and put my arm around her and held
her until she had cried everything she had.

That left only Francisco, standing alone, brave and tough as
a little matador. With the eyes of a child, still young enough to
question reality, he looked at Michael's body. Stef stood next to
Francisco. I saw Francisco's small hand reach out and clutch Stef's.
At that point I realized that nobody's pain would ever match that

of Francisco's. It was a pain that would last a lifetime, a tragedy that would sentence him back to the life of a peasant. Nature had reset his clock, had taken away his genie, had pulled him out of this wonderful dream. Too good a dream for a Mexican peasant boy, to dream like an American, to expect things so great that life—all of life—yes, both the present and the future, seem perfect. Too much to expect those kinds of dreams to exist and come true on such a little island, an insignificant little island.

About one thirty that morning, the hurricane hit with a vengeance. The wind was loud as a turbine. The rain was like bullets. We sat in a part of the shelter that Yvette and Nash had staked out. I wrapped myself in a blanket and shivered and stared straight ahead, ready for the hurricane. I had this image that we were on a plane that was going down, speeding to the ground. The pilot was telling us to fasten our seatbelts and put our head between our knees. In that moment of realization, you know there is nothing more you can do but wait, and you know this is not a dream from which at the last minute you will snap awake, sweaty but safe. So I waited. We all waited.

The shelter entrance was closed and bolted. Outside the building a cruel noisy hell had arrived. It battered the shelter as if to get at us like some grotesque hungry wolf. Pounding, pounding, beating at the door, clawing. The doors shook violently and then in one great burst the gates of hell snapped open. A wet wind tore throughout the room. Outside, the rabid storm raged. The whole world spun through the air, smashing against the shelter. Chaos orchestrated from hell.

The hurricane was now on top of us. It shook the shelter until the wooden beams of the ceiling creaked in pain. We were as trapped inside as we were outside. The ceiling shook more and more and I knew it would soon give in. Quickly, we moved people from the center of the shelter and crammed everyone against the walls of the concrete building. Just as the last person rushed to the side, half of the ceiling crashed to the floor and half of it was sucked like a toy kite into the air. Pieces of ceiling dangled from the roof and all at once a large chunk of concrete and wood flew across the room and pinned people onto the floor and against the wall. Screams louder than the hurricane itself filled the air. I couldn't look at what was happening, so I buried my face against my knees, knowing that nobody could get over to help those people because of the wind. One by one the crying and screaming stopped and their pain was over.

A few people crawled to those who were pinned under the broken piece of roof. Lifting what they could, they freed up some of the bodies. One small child and an old man survived, nearly unhurt. But the rest, fourteen in all, died almost instantly.

In three hours, the wind let up and the rain tapered off just a little. It was still too dangerous to move about, so we sat for three more hours—cramped and stiff and wet—sick deep, deep inside.

By daybreak we saw part of the sky for the first time. Around noon we left the shelter and went into town and stared at the brutality with which Mujeres had been raped.

We crept through the island—streets still full of water, windows shattered. Muddy sand oozed from the houses and shops. A boat of reporters pulled up to the island. People piled out and buzzed in every direction. A reporter from Miami began asking about the hurricane. We turned away, but he persisted, following us with two photographers. One asked if we had any film of the hurricane.

"Why don't you blokes just go to hell," Yvette roared.

"We just want a story," one of them said. "What's wrong with that?"

"I can tell you what's wrong with that. Just go fock yourself. And you too," Nash said, ready to attack the cameraman.

The reporter continued, "We're just reporting the news. Can you tell us what it was like...what happened?"

"Can't you see what happened?" I said.

We kept walking, but the men dragged after us. "We heard some people died. Is it true? How many people died? Were they Mexicans or what?"

With that, Stef reeled around and took a wide swipe at the reporter, catching him on the chin, snapping his head back. The photographer took a picture of Stef in his dirty rain-soaked jacket and matted hair. Nash leaped for the photographer and yanked the camera from his hand. He wheeled it over his head like a lasso and flung it to the ground. It ruptured into a dozen pieces of glass and metal; the film popped out. The photographer raved about having us thrown in jail and making us pay for the camera. We walked away, heading for the La Hamaca.

We held a small service for Michael, then gathered his things, whatever was of value, and left them with Rodriguez the mayor to give to Michael's mother when she came from San Cristobal.

All day people came to the island, each with their own special interest, or just to see the raw death and the broken lives. These people, these human leeches, some from Cancun, stood and gazed and pointed from a safe distance, taking pictures of Mujeres down on her knees. No doubt this would become the talk, the highlight, of their Caribbean vacation—the first thing mentioned on Monday morning back at the office.

Then, too, people came to help. The Red Cross set up a small clinic where the church used to be. From there they treated the wounded and handed out food and clean water and shot the islanders with a booster for typhoid. We helped the town people as they attempted to put Mujeres back together. Late in the evening, we went to the back of the island and made camp under the stars.

A bright sun came up the next morning. The sea was calm and the sky was as blue as a new car. The clouds were soft and white. It was a nice day, but we were all too sick inside to enjoy it. I felt betrayed with that sense of betrayal that lovers get, and nothing, no matter how sweet, could make the feeling go away.

The ferry ride back to the mainland was quiet. All of us stared ahead in silence.

A bus was going south to Tulum. We didn't think very long before getting on. We didn't really give a damn where it was going.

Yvette leaned against me and held my arm. "The hurricane was so terrible," she said. "I'll never forget it. I thought for a while we were all going to die. I thought you and Stef would never come back. I felt so empty."

The bus rolled past the flat scruffy Yucatan coast. The air was hot and there was no island breeze to cool us. The sweaty breath of the tropics filled the bus as we rode down the edge of Mexico.

What a bus ride it was! More than all the others, this one was etched into my memory because it came after my soul had been tested as never before in the wake of the hurricane, and Michael's death, and the night at the shelter.

As we rode on, there was a part of my wounded spirit not yet healed. I felt an inner conflict. For the first time in my life I had a fear of the future—a trace, yes—but fear, nonetheless. And yet one part of me felt stronger than ever before. That was the conflict. And it was this bus, this stupid slow dirty bus that dragged me into the future, delivered me to tomorrow, and was in some way part of that fear.

All my life I thought I could anticipate and be ready for the future—tomorrow, next week, whenever. But that was in a life where things were controlled and events were constructed, where I was the architect of my life—or so I believed. Then take that person who thinks he knows his future and put him in a world where nothing can be predicted and where the future goes berserk right before your eyes. I was thinking about all the things I should have considered long ago. As we bumped down the pock-scarred road to Tulum, I stared squarely ahead, looking hard, very hard, into the future. I came to the conclusion that what we learn in this world has no particular relationship to the length of time spent learning it, and therefore, my short two months of traveling was already a lifetime. In the past, I expected satisfaction and happiness to roll effortlessly towards me—to learn about life and to discover its meaning any way I could. I had searched through books and sat in classrooms—spent time in so many lecture halls and galleries of knowledge. But I was just flying low over the surface of what needed to be learned, skimming over it but touching none of it. Now, finally, I had found life. I didn't understand all of it yet, but I knew where it was and how to reach it. I thought back to life on 35th Street on the west side of Chicago, and then to my life in Baltimore as a student. Life in those places was all right, yet I never felt the way I did now rattling down the road, the four of us, in a tinny old bus.

Yet on the very same bus, a wonderful thing happened. Sitting next to me, riding quietly, sullen, torn by the hurricane, Yvette said not a word as we rode through miles of coastal jungle—said nothing at all for a long time. Too filled with the sad silence and the quick memory of the past. She reached over and touched my arm. "Alex?" she said.

I turned, "Yeah, Yvette."

"Alex, I love you very, very much."

Spontaneously, I said, "I love you, too, Yvette." I turned and stared again at the front of the bus, into the future, until finally Yvette's words and my answer to them pulled me out of my dead stare and I looked again at Yvette. "What did you just say?"

Unflinchingly, Yvette said, "I love you, Alex...very, very much."

When Yvette said that, something spun inside me. I wasn't threatened by her feelings as I might have been at other times in my life. I wanted her to love me because I wanted to be in love with her. I wanted all the goodness I saw in Yvette to be mine—not to own it but to cherish it. And then if I was lucky, I could give some of that goodness back to her. If I was very lucky and if I tried very hard, I could do that, I hoped. The last small piece of the future still in my control.

CHAPTER SEVEN

August 9, 1980 – Day 68

Tulum was not a town, it was just a spot on the map. A small cluster of Mayan ruins. The ruins themselves are nice, though not especially magnificent. But because they sit on the very edge of a high cliff over the Caribbean, there is a special beauty to them. We wandered about the ruins and Stef photographed a little until the sun was almost down and it was time to find a place to spend the night. Nash suggested the beach. One of the Mexicans told us about a small farm a mile or so up the road where we could put up our hammocks and buy dinner from the farmer. A black night fell quickly over Tulum.

We walked down the road. "I can't see anything," I said. "I can't even see my feet below me."

"I don't think this is safe," Nash said. "Someone could jump out of the bushes. Or an animal could get us, maybe."

"I've got my knife out," Yvette said, holding a hunting knife as long as her arm.

"Are you sure this is the right way?" Nash asked. "It's so dark, we're sitting targets for anything. Jaguars are all over here, you know."

Stef took a flashlight from his pack; it was little good against the murkiness around us. "This must be Mayan darkness," Stef said. "Maybe that's why they came to Tulum—to search out the night and find its deep secrets."

We walked on, slowly, as if toward the end of the Earth. We pulled together until we were shoulder to shoulder. Yvette said, "Look, there's a light ahead." Like June bugs, we went after the light. It was a small house next to a neat field of pineapples. The owner agreed to let us camp on a patch of grass near the field. In the morning we toasted bread and cooked eggs that we bought from the farmer, and we ate a pineapple from his grove. Stef went off for an hour to photograph but said little when he returned. He seemed to have lost much of his usual enthusiasm. By noon we were on another wretched bus going south to Chetumal, a town that sits on the border between Mexico and Belize.

At Chetumal, we went straight to the border of Belize, the only English-speaking country in Central America—a country inhabited mostly by descendants of Africans who settled in the jungles after a flotilla of slave ships crashed on a coral reef long ago. Later, England established a colony there, calling it British Honduras. Eventually, it was granted independence and took up a new name.

For weeks while traveling on the Gringo Trail, we had been warned about going to Belize. "They don't like druggers and dopers," people said, and "Long hair and a beard is a ticket to trouble in Belize." Based on those reports, we were in for tough times, looking as rag-tag as we did. "They will check your money at the border and stamp your passport for how long you can stay based on how much money you have."

We made preparations as best we could. We combed our hair and put on clean clothes and divided our money so that we all had about the same amount, hoping no one would be sent back. The border consisted of a small river that ambled through the jungle. On the north side was an adobe building, the Mexican checkpoint. On the south side was a cinderblock building, the Belizean checkpoint.

We walked out of Mexico across a footbridge over a brown river and into Belize. We were the only ones crossing at that time. At the checkpoint, a young, very serious Belizean said in slow Caribbean English, "May I have your pa-a-a-h-h-s-ports please? Where are you going?

I said, "Through Belize to Guatemala."

"May I see your checks?" he asked, meaning traveler's checks. He counted each packet as carefully as a bank teller might and stamped our passports and shooed us on. Another Belizean dug through our packs, but only superficially. All in all, it went fine.

By the time we got through the checkpoint, it was towards the end of a miserably hot day. We looked around for which way to go. There was little to decide. A narrow road cut ahead into the jungle. We started walking as the sun settled down behind low leafy trees. The second the sun was gone, droves of mosquitoes flared up in great swarms from out of the brush, tearing savagely into us.

"Oh, Christ!" Yvette screamed. "Mosquitoes! Tons of them!"

A thick fog of buzzing bugs descended on us, attacking with no respect for eyes or lips or any other exposed part.

"Get the repellent!" someone yelled.

"Where is it? Who's has it?" I screamed. "Oh, God, quick!" Stef tore open the top of his pack. Clothes and things flew out in handfuls. At last…the precious can. The swarm was thicker than ever. Stef sprayed the air around us, clearing the clot of insects—though much, much too late.

There were no two ways about it, we had to get out of the jungle. Down the road we sped, walking as fast as we could. A car roared up behind us—an old Chevrolet, beat to hell but beautiful as heaven. We stood in the road blocking it, waving for mercy. As soon as the car stopped, we climbed in, ready and happy to be going anywhere we could.

"To Corozal Town's where I'm goin'," the Belizean driver said.

"So are we," I replied quickly, not having any idea where it was.

Corazol had the look of something out of a western movie set. Boardwalks in place of sidewalks. Old wooden buildings with balconies that stretched out over the boardwalk onto a street of dirt and mud. We entered a hotel through swinging saloon-style doors that opened into the lobby.

Later in the evening we sat in the lobby and drank cold beer. Nash was obsessed with the saloon doors. Pretending to be John Wayne, he came bursting into the lobby, pushing the doors open. Upper lip curled, he stared around the room as if hunting for the bad guys. He did this again and again, swaggering into the hotel stiff-legged, hands at his hips. In his French accent, he said, "I'll give ya whon chance to draw yer gun, par-ner, 'fore I send ya ta

Boot Hill!" With that, he yanked an imaginary pistol from his side, shot several times, and blew smoke from the tip of his index finger. It was damn funny.

CHAPTER EIGHT

August 11, 1980 – Day 70

By ten o'clock the next morning, we had made our way to Belize City on the coast of the Caribbean.

Some years previously, I remember reading in James Michener's book, *The Drifters*, about advice for travelers. Things like "Always do your laundry whenever you can," "Never refuse sex," "Never play poker with anyone named Doc," and "Never eat at a restaurant called Mom's." It was good advice, all but for the warning about a restaurant named Mom's, because if for some reason you found yourself in Belize City, there were two things to do. First, ask for directions to the Swing Bridge. Second, when you got there, go to Mom's restaurant. A large plain clapboard building—the home of the best food in the entire hemisphere. All the moms in the world couldn't do a better job at any price, let alone what Mom's charged.

We sat at a wooden table that had years of wear scratched into it. Mom's was a big place—big and open and plain as can be. We ordered fried chicken with potatoes and coleslaw and, thank God, no tortillas. We ate like starving people, stopping only to order another Pelican beer, a locally brewed concoction that came in green bottles with no label. It had the kick of gin. Someone at Mom's even said they douse it with gin at the brewery to give it character. Character—shit! That stuff had an entire personality!

Once again, we were in one of those lost hideouts on the back of the world. Weird, ignored, forgotten. Mom's was a little like the train station in Palenque with its covey of world vagabonds, and just like in Palenque, all around us was a flurry of languages.

In a thick German accent, the man at the next table said, "Vare are you going?" He and his friend were eating Mom's chicken. They were tanned dark as chocolate and weather worn. They had been on the road a very long time, I figured.

"We aren't sure where we're going," Nash said, stuffing potatoes and coleslaw into his mouth. "We might just stay here and eat zis focking chicken forever."

"We've came from Caye Caulker," the German said. "It's an island." He pointed out beyond the restaurant. "If you want a good place with no madness, that's where you should go."

"Well, we were on an island off the Yucatan," Yvette said. "We got hit by a hurricane. I'm not sure I want that again."

The Germans said they were going north up to the Yucatan and we told them about Tulum and Isla Mujeres and more about the hurricane. We told them how to get to Chichen Itza and Merida and I realized that what Miles had said about the Gringo Trail back in San Miguel was now true—we were encountering the modern-day pioneers passing along the Trail. We told the Germans what to watch for as they traveled up the Gringo Trail.

All in all, there seemed not much to do in Belize City but get high. Dope, more than anything, was the main commodity and everyone was selling it or buying it. An odd thing considering the prognostications that Belize does not tolerate drugs.

"Cocaine, mahn. Cocaine here," said a man outside Mom's.

A tall skinny Belizean came up to us. "You going to Caye Caulker, mahn?"

"We don't know," I said.

"Where you from?"

"All over," I said.

"The US?"

"Me and him." I pointed to Stef.

"And she?" he asked.

"*She*...is from Australia," Yvette snipped.

"An Aussie. Okay, mahn," the Belizean said. "I can get you out to Caulker. And I can get you some good dope to take along. You want reefer, mahn? I can do it, I can. How much you want? I get you each a nickel bag," he said. "Five dollars American. It's safe on Caulker. You don't believe me? Ask the Germans."

As the Germans came out of Mom's, the Belizean said, "Tell the Gringos here it's okay to go to Caulker and to bring dope, too."

"Yah, it's fine," one of the Germans said. "Very safe."

"We don't know if we want to go," I said. We gathered together to talk about it. Stef said he wanted to go in spite of the hurricane on Mujeres. Yvette said it was probably all right. Nash said nothing, so we decided to go to Caye Caulker. Stef went with a Belizean to get the stash.

We sat outside Mom's on orange crates and watched Belize City slow boil in the afternoon tropical sun. Stef was gone a long while. In the meantime, the Belizean with the boat said to Nash,

"Where you from, mahn?"

Nash looked away, turning his nose to the sky, not wanting to be bullied by the Belizean. He leaned against the wall and lit a cigarette.

But the Belizean persisted. "I know you, mahn. You're from France."

Nash steamed slowly under the inquisition, but the more Nash ignored him, the more the Belizean pushed.

"Well, I don't like no Frenchman, and I don't like you. I don't take no frogs to Caulker. No way, mahn, no way!"

That did it. Nash flipped the stub of his cigarette into the street and looked at the Belizean. "Fock you! I wouldn't ride in your smelly little boat if it was the last one in the ocean." He turned sharply and went into Mom's.

The Belizean stood his ground. He looked at Yvette. "I don't like no frogs."

Stef returned stoned. He showed us his score. A mammoth bag of fine-looking reefer. A bargain beyond belief. "This whole damn country's loaded with the stuff," Stef chuckled.

"Let's go," Yvette said. "Get Nash."

I went inside Mom's and found him sitting at one of the tables. We went back out but as soon as Nash came from Mom's, the Belizean started up. "Told you, I don't take no frogs."

Before Nash could explode with a string of fock yous, Yvette exploded like a cherry bomb. "Well then you listen to this," she said to the Belizean, "and you listen bloody well. Either you take all of us or none of us. If you ain't going to take us, then just pack it in. We don't bloody well give a damn. You got the only fucking boat in all of Belize, do you?"

Stef pushed Nash and Yvette into a neutral corner away from the Belizean. Stef said, "Let's just hold off on going to Caulker. We'll get a room and go tomorrow, okay? Or maybe we won't go at all. What difference does it make?"

When the Belizean heard this, his tune changed. He sensed the trip was off and he quickly said, "Okay, I take you all. Maybe it's been a hot day in Belize, you know."

We got into the Belizean's small outrigger sailboat and took to the water—no engine, just a single sail. Twice we floated idly out on the sea as the Belizean waited for the wind to kick up again. Each time, he lit a joint and passed it around. Finally, out before us a humble little island came into view. The Belizean coasted to the shore of Caye Caulker. "This is it, mahn," he said.

We climbed out and waded through knee-deep water to the island—Robinson Crusoe being delivered to paradise. The sun was hot, but the island looked peaceful and calm and perfect. A beautiful speck of land in a turquoise sea. There were no obvious stores or shops or cafés. No hotels, no high-rise apartments, no condominiums. Just a few fishing boats and a small dock and some huts with thatched roofs sitting up on stilts. A sandy path weaved its way into the island.

"It's wonderful 'ere," Yvette shouted. "I want to take all my clothes off and run around and dive in the sea."

"You better wait a while for that," Nash admonished. "We don't know anything about this focking island. Or what kind are the focking people who live here."

We walked to the center of the island. Yvette did her directional thing, turned, and pointed. We followed until we came to a house near the end of the island that, unlike the scattering of small shacks and huts, was a regular down-to-earth place made of plain clapboard siding. A handful of people sat on the front porch. A green parrot strutted pompously back and forth across the railing.

"We're looking for a place to say," Stef said.

"You can stay here, I suspect," said a man.

"Whose place is this?"

"Mrs. Reeves," he said. "She rents rooms."

"Where is she?"

"Inside." He pointed over his shoulder.

We walked into the house, through a dining room and into the kitchen. There, next to the sink, a large teapot of a woman was peeling potatoes. Before we got a word out, she said, "I have just one room left. Y'all can have it if you want it."

"How much?" Stef asked.

"Dollar-fifty a night…American. For each, that is," she answered, almost as an apology. She looked back and scanned us quickly, then returned to the potatoes. "Breakfast is every day at eight-thirty…ninety cents. Dinner is five o'clock, a buck twenty-five. You don't have to take the meals if you don't want to. You can cook out back for nothing."

We paid the fee. Mrs. Reeves showed us to the room. It was simple but good-sized: four cots, one small table, two windows, one to the east and one to the south. It had a good view of the sea and a nice breeze.

CHAPTER NINE

August 12, 1980 – Day 71

Life has different meaning to different people, but to all of us its meaning changes across time. In fact, it changes a little each day, each minute. These shifts and swells in meaning are moved by events around us, some obvious and fast, some slow and quiet.

Love is like that. Sometimes falling in love begins unexpectedly on the street as two people pass, as two eyes meet. Other times it grows out of a fragile seed that no one quite remembers planting. It starts as a shaky skinny twig, so vulnerable to the harsh hands and rough feet of the world. But as if by a miracle, a tree grows strong and tall and good. That kind of love is hard to cut down or kill. It needs only to be nourished and it will thrive, and each year it will blossom again so that even in old age it remains full of life.

Like most people, I've had many different kinds of love. Fast sweaty love pounded out in the bedroom until its goodness was spent and its fruits plucked, as if devoured in starvation. Then, satisfied, it was gone. I've had love that started slowly with grand and good intentions but died a paltry death.

When I looked at Yvette, something inside me fluttered. I saw things about her I hadn't seen in the beginning. I wondered, does love give us an extra sense that focuses on only one person and lets us see a little into their soul—the most private part of this thing human? It felt good and at the same time wrong. Wrong because I was caught in life's vise—squeezed between the love of two people. Simmering in the memory of a lover I had left behind and fed by the sweetened nourishment of another. I was choked with feelings of guilt that come from deep within when we try to love two people. I told myself it was impossible to love two people in exactly the same way. That's what I kept telling myself.

The days on Caulker flipped by like the pages of a good book. Each day after breakfast, Stef went to the reef that comes up to the edge of the island. There, he would snorkel and dive down into the crystal waters. Most of the time Nash went along. They would ride with Nigel, one of the Belizean islanders, who had a small dugout canoe.

Yvette and I hid out on the tiny island and swam in the calm pure waters, running along its beaches. She'd dive into the gentle surf, swimming in and out like a porpoise. I'd followed her into the warm sea. We would spin through the water the way we had done on Isla Mujeres off Garafon.

One day, lying on the sand, Yvette said, "Alex, this all has to come to an end sometime, doesn't it? I mean it can't go on forever. Can it? Can we live forever on this tropical island and swim in the Caribbean. And eat fish and crab and lobster every night?"

I looked up at Yvette. The sun shone behind her; her body was only an iridescent silhouette. She knelt on the ground next to me with one of her quick cat-like moves. Her body rubbed against mine. We were both dark as acorns, our skin smooth as scrubbed leather. Her brown hair had shreds of blonde from months in the sun. It fell across her face and chest. Her soft eyes were beautiful.

"I don't know anything anymore," I said. "I don't know what I should do or shouldn't do. Down here, there's nothing you *have* to do." I drew Yvette close to me. "Yvette, I love you. That much I know. In the past two months everything I once knew and believed has been altered. You and Stef and Nash are the only people that make sense to me."

"We're good together, Alex," Yvette said. "I know you had a lover back home. I had one too in Sydney. But he was different from you, Alex."

"And you're different from all the women in the world."

"Do you ever worry that maybe this will end between us?"

"I don't want it to," I said.

"I don't either, but I worry about it."

"I love you," I said.

"Oh, I love you, Alex. More than ever."

"Then it won't end. If you love me and I love you, how can it end?"

Yvette rolled on top of me and we turned and rolled in the sand until we were on the edge of the warm waters of the sea. I held Yvette in my arms and felt the tight muscles of her body. We swam in the water and then went back to Mrs. Reeves. It was still early in the afternoon. We had the room to ourselves for hours.

CHAPTER TEN

As the Gringo Trail goes, Caye Caulker was nothing more than a filling station. But like all the places along the Trail, it was a concoction of odd and somewhat misfitted people. That's how it was with Lou and Len, two Americans who rented a room at Mrs. Reeves's. They spent their days on the porch, feet on the railing, watching the ocean, drinking Pelican beer.

I came to know Len pretty well. He was one of those people who talked to anybody near him, and when he couldn't do that, he talked to the parrot, and when the parrot left, he just talked to himself.

Lou never spoke much. He had a tooth missing in the front of his mouth and he was very conscious of it. What's more, Lou had a thing for Yvette that was immediately obvious. I'd sit on the porch with Len and Lou, listening to Len ramble. Yvette would come by wearing her bikini and sit on my lap and put her arm around my shoulder. Lou would fidget like a cat.

In time, Len told me about what he and Lou were doing in Central America on this forgotten island in a corner of the Caribbean. They were so different from the others on the island, I had been wondering about it for a long time.

Len leaned toward me and proudly said, "Okay, Alex, here's the story. We're in the dope business." He looked around the porch, gleaning the area for unwanted ears. He leaned closer and in hardly a whisper said, "We have cocaine."

"*Whoa,*" I said. "Cocaine!"

Len beamed proudly. "We get it in Columbia."

"How much cocaine?"

"A lot." Len looked around again. "Five kilos. Pure snow, virgin stuff. Five kilos."

"*Holy shit!*" I said.

"Here's the trick. We get the stuff in Columbia, like I said. Then we take boats up the coast until we reach Belize. From here we fly to the US."

"On your own plane, I guess."

"Oh, hell no. We take a regular flight from Belize City."

"What about customs?"

"Just walk right through."

"Cut it out. You guys are full of shit," I said, tilting back in my chair.

"No, Alex, it's true." Len sat straight up and again said, "I'm telling you, it's true. Wanna see the stuff…the coke?"

Lou pushed Len back with an elbow and looked at me square in the eye and started explaining how they did it. "See, we have two backpacks that are exactly the same. *Exactly.* One has the dope and a bit of clothes. The other has all our real clothes. We check both packs on the plane in Belize City, and we get a claim ticket for each of them. Belize don't give a shit what you take out of the country—they never look. In the US, we pick up the pack with the dope. Mostly, they just flag us through. But if they tell us to open the pack and find the stuff, we act real surprised and confused, that sort of thing, and say, 'Hey, wait, this ain't ours. Look, here's our claim ticket, see?' And we pull out the clothes from the pack with the dope and there's all sorts of shit that ain't ours, like women's bras and crap like that. Then we say, `Look, over there, there's our pack.' And we get the pack that's sitting in the corner and show 'em the claim ticket. Course they get real fucked up pissed thinking they been had, but it ain't nothing they can do. Pretty good, huh? They only stopped us once coming into Miami. But we got off. They couldn't prove shit. That's why we don't go through Miami no more. We've been through New Orleans six times now and never got caught. Pretty smooth, huh, Alex?"

"Pretty smooth."

Well, Lou and Len didn't look like big-time drug runners, not the kind I expected anyway. But I guess that's why they'd been so lucky till now. Later Len showed me their stash—a giant block of coke.

Several days on, Len told me about another scam he and Lou used to make money in Latin America. This one involved selling American passports on the black market.

"We get ten grand for each one," Len said, "and we usually sell ten or twenty at a time. Legitimate ones, not phony ones. Here's how." And again there was a little huddle on Mrs. Reeves porch as Len went through the details. "We start out in graveyards back in the States. We find someone about our age who died young. 'Course they gotta have a Spanish name. Then we get a copy of their birth certificate and we get a social security number in their name. When we get all that crap, we go to the passport office and apply for a new passport with a picture and all. A few weeks later, bam, a brand-new passport! Then we fly down here to Guatemala or El Salvador or Peru. Peru's a good place to sell passports. We always deal in cash. We sell the passport, the birth certificate and the social security card, and just like that they're an American citizen. All they have to do is replace the picture, but that's easy if you get someone who knows what he's doing. Pretty smooth, huh, Alex?"

"Yeah, Len, pretty smooth. You guys must be millionaires by now," I said.

"Nah…we spend a lot of it, y'know," Len said.

"Yeah, we spend a lot of it," Lou confirmed.

To look at Len and Lou, you couldn't imagine they made that kind of money, especially Lou with his missing tooth.

⅄

After some time on Caulker, I came to the conclusion that the world is made of two kinds of people. The first are those who are running to something—the seekers, the searchers, the hunters. The second are those running away from something—the quitters, the abandoned, the hunted—those looking to lose their past. They were all there on Caye Caulker. Funny that people in search of opposite things would cross paths in the same remote place. Perhaps there was something similar in what each sought. After all, running to something is really the same as running away from something because to run toward a thing requires that you move farther away from something else. And yet, there are those who don't seem to be moving in any direction, forward or back. It seemed to be so with Dauphine.

That evening when Stef and Nash returned from the reef, we went to Freddie's, a place on the island that served as its tavern. Not much of a place really, just a few bare wooden tables, cold Pelican beer, some rum, some Coca-Cola, an old tarnished chess set, and a backgammon game. Inside Freddie's, the rich tinny sound of Caribbean music sprung from a cheap stereo.

Stef told me about three American women he and Nash had met that afternoon. They had all gone to the reef in Nigel's boat. The women were college friends now scattered about, two living in Philadelphia, one in San Diego. Stef talked voraciously about the one named Dauphine, describing her as if he had known her his whole life. He talked about her with that same intensity that photography brought to his soul.

Dauphine and her two friends came to Freddie's. She was pretty but not unusually so; she had a certain California look I'd seen before. There was a serene appearance that she projected, though it wasn't until later that I found how easy it is to be fooled by that.

It was a blistering hot night. With no hope to sleep for hours, we sipped Pelican beer mixed half and half with Coca-Cola the way it's done in the tropics. A strange concoction, for sure, but not as bad as it sounds. The cola keeps you hydrated, cutting through the morning hangover. The only thing worse than a sleepless night in the tropics is a sweaty hangover the next day.

Len and Lou also came to Freddie's that night. I could tell

they had dipped into their cocaine and I wondered how much would be left by the time they made it back to New Orleans. Lou stared at Yvette perpetually—her strange, crazy, uniquely beautiful features must have carved a sensational image on his cocaine-soaked brain. Yvette had that effect on people, on me for sure. Sometimes, just to look at her was such a pleasant experience, it was difficult to stop. Beauty that was simple, pure, and natural. I kept seeing parts of it I'd never seen before. Eyes, green like the Caribbean. Yet like the sea, there were traces of blue and hazel and azure all mixed in. Eyes that were full of mystery and excitement and passion. The eyes of a sorcerer that could penetrate your soul. Eyes that were themselves a dimension of their own, a sixth, a seventh, and an eighth dimension. I watched Lou look at her, unable to pull away.

Finally, Lou broke from his rigid stare and challenged everyone to backgammon. One of Dauphine's friends took him on. They played three quick games that Lou won as if by habit. Then Nash played Lou and again it was all Lou's, one after another.

It made Nash mad as hell that a hillbilly from some holler in Appalachia could beat him at backgammon. I didn't play because I'd never won a game of backgammon in my life; it would have been a frustrating experience for everyone. Next, Yvette played Lou, and for a while it looked as though she might win, though I'm sure it was only the distraction of playing Yvette that caused Lou to falter until, at the end, he came back with a quick win. He also beat Freddie, and a Swedish guy, and a Belgian woman. Lou loved the attention and the glory of it all; he smiled with a big gap-toothed grin.

Very late, we went back to Mrs. Reeves. All but Stef. He and Dauphine took off through a cluster of coconut palms toward the beach.

CHAPTER ELEVEN

August 15, 1980 – Day 74

Breakfast at Mrs. Reeves was itself worth the trip to Caye Caulker. It was served on a big table family style every morning at eight-thirty or so. First you got a pot of hot fresh coffee. Toast, butter, and marmalade were set on the table. Scrambled eggs and fried potatoes were brought out—eggs scrambled with chunks of fresh lobster! I had never eaten lobster like that, served almost as a condiment for flavoring. That's how it was. Breakfast was a slow event, as you might imagine, and on those days when Nash and Stef were up and out early, Yvette and I had the room to ourselves. We'd make love with just a meek breeze of sea air flowing into the room, and then after that we'd have breakfast. On those mornings, life was as perfect as it could possibly be.

One day at the table after breakfast, I said to Stef, "Yvette and I talked last night about leaving Caulker soon."

"How soon?" Stef asked.

"Very soon. Don't forget we need to be out before our visas expire."

"I'm not ready to leave yet," Stef said. "There's a lot more to do here. I want to dive some more and photograph. Besides, it's cheap here, and pretty damn nice. Why leave?"

"Well, you know, sooner or later we have to leave."

"Which way are you going?"

"To Guatemala."

Stef looked out the window at the blue Caribbean. He drank coffee and stared indifferently, but I could tell a hundred thoughts were flying through his mind.

"Well, how long do you want to stay?" I asked.

"I don't know…maybe a week. Maybe longer."

"A *week*! Our visas expire in three days."

Stef said nothing.

"It's because of Dauphine, isn't it? But you just met her." I realized how foolish that sounded, and I wished I hadn't said it. Then to make things worse, I came out with, "Are you in love with her?"

"Of course not, Alex. What are you talking about? I just want to stay a while longer."

Mrs. Reeves brought more coffee.

"Stef, our visas expire in a few days," I repeated.

"Well, I'm thinking about getting mine extended. There's a guy on the island who can do it. Dauphine told me about him last night."

"You mean that fat pig who lives in the hut in the middle of the island?"

"He's the constable here."

"Oh, shit, come on, Stef! He's nothing but a big slob. He has no authority to do that. He's always drunk or stoned. He does coke all day with Lou and Len. Are you telling me you'd let him stamp your visa? It's bullshit. He's a phony. And then what? We get to the border and they throw our asses in the can for having expired papers. No gracias, amigo!"

"You don't have to do it, Alex. You don't have to do a fucking thing. I said I'm getting *my* papers extended. You can split any time you want. You and what's her name."

"Oh, so that's it, is it? Now we're getting at the truth. You think I want to split with Yvette. How the hell could you think that, Stef?"

"Cut the crap, Alex! You're so god-damned in love with her you don't even know what's happening anymore. Or am I wrong, Alex? Tell me I'm imagining that."

I stared momentarily at Stef. "Yeah, I love her. You've known that. This isn't the first time we've talked about it."

"It's the first time you told me you love her."

"So what? What the problem with that? You think I'm planning to ride off into the sunset with her? Is that it?"

"Well…aren't you?"

"No, dammit. You're not listening to me. I love Yvette, but that doesn't change a thing between us. It's still you and me and Nash and Yvette.

"I don't think so, Alex. A lot has changed. It's all different now."

"Well, that's not how I see it."

Stef looked out the window for a long while, then got up and left the house.

I caught up with Yvette as she lay stretched out on the sand near the water. Nigel's canoe was heading out to the reef with Stef and Nash and Dauphine. I knelt next to Yvette. "It's all screwed up," I told her. "Stef's mad about everything. He thinks we're leaving without him."

"But he can't think that. We only have a couple of days to be out of the country. What about that?"

"He says he can get his papers renewed here on Caulker. Dauphine told him he could."

"Alex, he's bloody crazy. You don't believe that, do you? If we do that, we'll all end up in jail. Think what that would be like here in Belize."

"I know, I know," I said, "but he won't listen. He's made up his mind to stay on Caulker." I sifted sand through my fingers into little piles. Yvette reached over and touched my hand.

"Well then maybe we should leave."

"Yvette. It's not that simple. I've traveled with Stef for months. I just can't throw up my hands and say, 'That's it, goodbye.' Stef is my only true friend in this world. We're brothers...blood brothers. I can't walk out on him. I can't."

"But what about us, Alex? Do you love me?"

"Of course I do...from the bottom of my soul."

"And I love you. Isn't that enough?"

"Do you want me to leave without Stef?"

"Well I don't want some idiot stamping our papers. That's ludicrous!"

I walked to the water and waded up to my knees. Looking out across the blue sea, I watched Nigel's canoe head toward the reef. I came back and stood next to Yvette. "Let's not get freaked out over this, all right?"

"I know what it is," Yvette said. "It's that bitch, Dauphine, isn't it? She's screwing this up for everyone."

"Now just a damn minute, Yvette. Are you trying to tell me that because Stef met someone he likes, this is all her fault? Funny, but that's exactly what he tried to say this morning about us."

"You mean about me."

I said nothing; Yvette knew what I meant.

"Oh, really! Well there's an answer to this whole problem. I came a damn long way all by myself, and I can go the rest the way by myself, if that's what you people want. Maybe that will solve everyone's problem, huh Alex? Then it would be just you and Stef again."

"For Christ's sake, will you listen to me! I love you, Yvette, why is that so difficult. I don't want you to leave. I just want to work this out. All right? Okay?"

Yvette started walking to the sea. She stopped, turned, and said, "Yes." Then ran to the water.

The next day was hellish. Nobody talked to anyone. Nash, who knew nothing about any of this, was confused by the weird silence. Yvette was cold and distant. Stef spent the day and the previous night with Dauphine until dinner time when they came to Mrs. Reeves. It wasn't a good time for a big family discussion at the dinner table with everyone else there.

After dinner, the four of us plus Dauphine ended up on the porch. We watched the sun burn itself out in a prism of colors as it dropped into the sea. When that was over Stef coldly said, "I'm getting my visa extended tomorrow."

Stef's words hung orphaned in the air. Dauphine said, "He

can get it done here on Caulker. Other people have done it. We met an English guy who had his extended for four weeks. People do it all the time."

There was a long silence. Yvette said, "I don't think it's a good idea, Stef. I don't give a damn what the Englishman did. There is no embassy or consulate here on Caulker. That guy has no authority to extend a visa, or—"

"Oh yes he does," Dauphine insisted. "He has permission to do it if he wants."

"Excuse me," Yvette said, eyes glaring. "I was talking to Stef...Stefan Kale. Is *your* name Stefan Kale?"

Dauphine sank into her chair, lip curled.

"Okay you two, cut it out," I ordered. "What I want to know from Stef is what you're going to do. Are you staying or leaving?"

"I'm staying, Alex, I already told you I am."

"Well, we're leaving. You know that, Stef, don't you?"

Stef said nothing.

"Do you understand we want you to come with us?" I tried, again.

Stef looked away.

I groaned. "I don't know what to say. I guess that's it."

"I guess so," Stef uttered.

"We're leaving in the morning. You can still come with us," Yvette said.

"He doesn't want to," Dauphine replied.

"Oh, fuck you!" Yvette screamed. She stormed off the porch.

I looked at the stiff stone figures sitting next to me and went to find Yvette.

Morning breakfast was a terrible affair. Stef had coffee and toast and retreated to the porch. Nash told Yvette that he was staying with Stef and that he would get his papers extended also. He didn't think it was risky.

We had located a small sailboat that would take us into Belize City. We gathered our things and walked out onto the porch. I tried one last time. "Do you want to come with us?"

Stef shook his head.

"What is it, Stef? What's wrong?"

"Nothing's wrong, Alex. Why are you making it like this?"

I threw my hands in the air and picked up my pack. Yvette slung her pack over her shoulder. Eyes misty, she looked tenderly at Stef. "I'm going to miss you."

Stef couldn't help but smile.

We walked to the boat, heaved our things on board, and climbed on. The sail was set to the morning breeze. We pulled out to sea in a smooth wide arc leaving Caulker behind us.

In Belize City, we went immediately to the bus station and boarded the first bus for Guatemala. I can't tell you anything about the bus ride through Belize because I remember none of it. I was filled with a thick sadness that chilled my veins and drugged my body. I barely recall Yvette riding next to me. By the time we arrived at the border, the bus was all but empty. For the first time on this short trip, I noticed the thick jungle that surrounded us.

Dusk arrived bringing long sinister shadows through the jungle. A simple wire fence separated the two countries. Behind the fence on the Guatemalan side was a large sign in English that said *BELIZE IS GUATEMALA*. A curious sign, indeed. We went through Belizean customs and walked down a narrow footpath into Guatemala and had our papers stamped at the guard station.

"Where can we spend the night?" I asked the border guard. He shrugged and looked out the window into the dark jungle, saying in effect, 'out there.'

"What about a bus?" I asked. "Can we get to a city tonight?"

"A las cinco, mañana en la mañana."

The next city was Flores, but the bus wouldn't come until early in the morning. "Sleep right here," he said again, pointing to the jungle by the border fence.

There was little else we could do. The tent went up. We made a bowl of rice cooked with jalapenos and tomatoes and onions that we ate with birotes and had with water from our canteens. I was so tired I couldn't stay awake long enough to finish my meal—exhausted from the jungle and the bus ride and most of all from the stress of the past two days. With no resistance, my body slipped into sleep.

CHAPTER TWELVE

August 18, 1980 – Day 77

Dark black night and then—suddenly—the tent is filled with light. I jump to my knees and claw at the tent door, frantic. Quick, unzip tent door. I look out. Yvette hunches on all fours. Watches, waits. "What, what?" she asks. "What is it? What's out there?"

"Men," I say. "A jeep and army people."

"What do they want?"

"I don't know. They're looking at us, I think." My heart pounds like a jackhammer. It's just the two of us. The two of us and the men, six or eight of them. I can't see real well, too much light on us. Big gun perched on the back of the jeep.

"They have a machine gun," I say to Yvette.

"A what?"

"You know, a big army gun."

I call to the men, "Que hacen?"

No answer.

I pull back inside the tent and sit next to Yvette. She clings to me. The light is too bright to look at even through the lining of the tent. Big spotlight moves, first to our left and then to our right, back and forth slowly. Again it settles its hard eye on us. A man speaks through a megaphone.

"Should we get out?" Yvette says.

"No!" I say. "Stay here. Make them come to us."

Perfect silence for thirty seconds or so. Then I hear a heavy rattling sound, like bicycle chains on metal. I hear talk, slow and deliberate. "Over this way," one man says. "Mas ala izquierda, mas ala izquierda." More chains, more silence. Too much silence. Like a string of Chinese firecrackers, the sound of machine gun fire fills the air. Piercing gunfire for five, maybe ten seconds, shooting directly over us and next to us. I hear pieces of the jungle snap away as the rounds rip through the bush. We plaster ourselves onto the tent floor. I feel Yvette's fingers dig into my back. "Alex, they're shooting at us!" Yvette says. "Oh, Jesus, stop!"

I can't speak, my breath pumps. My spine turns cold.

The gunfire ends. Yvette presses her head against my chest. Her voice shakes as she asks, "Are you all right?"

"Yes, I'm okay."

"Why are they shooting at us?"

"I don't know. Shhh."

The sound of chains, bullets being loaded. "Oh, shit, no."

Yvette curls into a ball. "I love you, Alex."

Gun spits rounds wildly around us. Light focuses on our tent. We must be an easy target. Bullets fly past the tent. One tears through the top of the tent, whistling as it rips neatly in and out of the fabric. Why do they miss us? Some kind of perverse torture-game until they decide when to finish it? To finish us? For a second time, there is silence and again our lives are suspended on a string. We sit helpless, waiting for that quick moment when a bullet tears through the tent, through me and Yvette and in a second it will be over and the tent will be torn to rags. In a week we will have been turned into fodder—lost, gone, ended in the empty jungles of Eastern Guatemala. I feel helpless, like a puppy, yet I have a strange sense of peace, thinking it will end like this—me and Yvette together in love.

The jeep's engine roars. The light goes out and once again we are in complete darkness. The men drive off. One calls out, "Adiooooos, amigos."

⅄

The jungle returned to its own noisy silence and only then did we move for the first time. I touched Yvette's wet face. We were both unhurt except for what it had done to our soul—torn open and humiliated by the sub-humanity of the soldiers.

"Alex," Yvette muttered, "what happened?" She lay on the floor of the tent in a pool of sweat. "Are you okay?" she kept asking.

I didn't know any more than she what had happened. And even if I did, those explanations have little meaning in the face of death. We had a difficult choice with almost no options. What to do? Go back into Belize? Little chance of getting in. We were in Guatemala—period. And so far, this seemed to be a hell of a hostile place.

"We'll pull through this, mate," Yvette said, in her tough, stiff-lipped way. "We'll make it through this. We'll make it through everything."

I felt the same sense of courage and strength that came to me after the hurricane while riding back to the shelter on Garafon. These people, whoever they were with their silly guns and deadly games, no longer scared me. I felt strength in my soul; it seemed to pour into me from Yvette, whose inner power and energy was at times overwhelming. It was her energy that powered mine, and together we were stronger than all the little boys in the world with all their little guns.

We slept in exhaustion until five in the morning when the bus for Flores arrived. For the second time that night, I leaped to my feet, nearly poking my head through the top of the tent. I opened the door and called urgently to the bus driver to wait for us. "Cinco minutos, por favor," I yelled in desperation. Why is it that in the afternoon the buses are three hours late but in the middle of the night they're perfectly on time?

Yet another sad bus in rural Central America. Small fragile looking men seated with portly wives. Children resting on their laps or sucking a teat for breakfast. And as always, the things destined for the market. Woven baskets, blankets, chickens, mangos, papaya, a cut of beef from some stringy bull.

The bus took us out of the night, away from the border and into the lowland forest of eastern Guatemala. We were now deep in the bowels of the jungle that sweeps down into Guatemala and Honduras. The heat from the rainforest hit us like a raging locomotive. Steamy traces of night mist clinging to the low bushes made the green-pastel plants appear as though viewed through a diffusion lens. We were all alone, Yvette and I, deep in the badlands of Central America where few people live. Where life is too tough for even the most durable. Where mankind is but another insignificant creature—a small trivial part of its ecology.

In the jungle, things can no longer be classified as good or bad. Rather, everything has its own level of intolerability, and that which is not intolerable becomes sufficient. One merely seeks a respite from the unendurable. From the torturous extremes of Nature. A reprieve from the heat of her inferno, her toothy insects, her biting plants and stinging vines. From spiders as big as a man's hand. From humidity that festers green fungus on everything. From all those things, which together can cause a mind to snap and leave it an empty helpless thing.

On these buses there were always one or two members of the National Guard. Young boys of sixteen or seventeen drafted from the towns and villages and issued a set of jungle fatigues and a carbine and nothing else. They were proud of their uniforms and their guns. And it was fun, I suppose, for once in their life to be someone special. It must have been wonderful until they realized they were clay pigeons for the bullets of the guerillas—the finely-trained, well-aimed, purposeful trigger of the revolutionaries. Then it was no longer fun. You could tell which ones knew this and which ones didn't. Now I knew what it was like to be used for target practice. I knew what that does to your world and your life and how it all looks afterward.

On the bus that morning, along with the Guatemalans, were two Gringos—the Carter brothers. Both were in their twenties, originally from Washington, DC, now farming with their father in the Yucatan near Vera Cruz. They spoke good Spanish and they knew Central America well. They had come to sell a used car in Belize where the demand for cars was great. But, like us, they had to leave the country through a different place from where they entered. This meant passing through Guatemala on the Gringo Trail and circling back up to Mexico and over to the Yucatan.

One of the Carters explained that Belize and Guatemala have been at war for more than a hundred years. "You see, those men weren't shooting at you. They were shooting across the border at Belize...at the whole damn country. It goes on constantly."

"Well, they put a bullet through our tent," Yvette said.

"They were just bored," Carter said, shrugging it off casually. "Every night they go there and empty their guns into the darkness. Pretty silly, huh? You guys just made their nighttime duties a little more fun, that's all."

The other Carter told us that the dispute between the countries was about a road that never got built. "You see, at one time Belize was a part of Guatemala. Then the Brits came by and made a deal with Guatemala saying they would build a road through the jungle that would connect the east coast with the cities of Western Guatemala. If the Brits did that, Guatemala would give them all the land that is now Belize. The English wanted it because of the hardwoods and the fruit. The way the Guatemalans saw it, they didn't really give a damn about the eastern half of their country because it was colonized by Africans who didn't have much in common with the Guatemalans. But the Brits never built the road—they just took the country and called it British Honduras. After many years, the Brits gave independence to British Honduras and the name was changed to Belize. *But* since the road was never built, Guatemala claims that Belize still belongs to her."

"That's why the big sign that says Belize is Guatemala," the other Carter explained.

We talked to the Carters as the bus jolted through the jungle. The morning mist was now all but gone. The green jungle clung in all its glory so close to the rutted road that leaves swept against the side of the bus when we swung around a corner or when the road thinned to a single strand. The jungle was speckled with flowers that burst into a blast of colors against the primary green backdrop—a thick, tall jungle all the way to the top of the zapote trees where the spider monkeys clustered in safety as they danced from tree to tree. A gust of warm air blew into the bus.

Around mid-morning we arrived at the small village of Flores, from there we would go to Tikal, the venerable capital of the ancient Mayan empire stuffed far away deep in the Guatemalan jungle. This was it—Tikal, with all its mystery and glory and wonder, its massive pre-Columbian temples. And somewhere there, I believed, were the answers to all my questions. Now after hundreds of miles on rotted buses, crowded trains, desert paths, sweaty jungles, tropical islands, now we were but a few kilometers from that one singular, important, eclectic place. There was nothing more to wait for. No more delays. Nothing more to plan for. There was only the final anticipation of getting there. The only thing to do was to go directly and quickly to Tikal. All the preliminary thoughts and plans had been made across the miles and miles of my mind.

We poked around Flores, hunting for a ride to Tikal. A man with an old truck said he could take us most of the way. We climbed on the back. Soon, the truck stopped; the driver pointed to a path in the jungle. It wasn't long before we came to a clearing and a small hut next to which was a trivial little airstrip just barely big enough for a cub plane. Outside the hut was an open hearth with a pot of simmering beans. Hungry smells filled the air. Farther on there was a clearing, a few cabanas, a couple of tents and hammocks. The ghost of an old fire sent a wisp of smoke up into the trees. The camp was deserted except for someone curled in a hammock. He watched us like a cat spying an intruder, gradually leaning his head over the side of the hammock, saying nothing, merely watching as we walked closer. We stopped at a safe distance and, from there, I said, "Perdoname, Señor, buscarmos un lugar acampar por la noche."

The man rose in his hammock and dangled his feet over the side. He rubbed his eyes and pushed hair out of his face. "I suppose you can stay here," he said.

Yvette asked, "Can we put up our tent?"

"You can do anything you damn well like," he said, "You're in the jungle now." He stood up, shuffled around the camp, and came over and looked at us with a level of suspicion, then held his hand out and said, "Name's Ryan."

I shook the hand of a farmer or a carpenter, rough calluses with skin like hide. Ryan walked over to a jug of water, scooped a ladle full, splashed it on his face, and poured the rest over his head. "Must take a bath every day in the jungle," he grunted.

"Who lives here?" Yvette asked.

"Who lives here?" he repeated. "We do, that's who. The archeologists who work on the ruins," Ryan's hand panned in the direction.

"Archeologists?" I asked.

Ryan grunted a second time. "I'm head of a team." He sat in a canvas chair. "Apologies, I don't normally look like this."

I sensed an accent in Ryan's speech. New England, perhaps, rural New England or possibly Cambridge, Massachusetts, but toned down a bit as if lost to time.

"And we weren't exactly expecting visitors. As you can imagine, there's not a hell of a lot to do out here in the jungle at night, not when you're here for two months at a stretch. No electricity, just kerosene lamps...get the picture?" He looked around the camp in search of something. "There is, however, one thing to do. There's the little bastard." He pointed to an empty bottle of tequila, used, spent, discarded—lying by the remains of the fire, flung there from Ryan's hammock no doubt. "We had a little party last night. That's how it goes. Don't do it too very often, but occasionally," Ryan said, walking around. "Anyone for coffee?"

We declined. Too hot to drink coffee at mid-morning in the tropics, clothes pasted to my back and legs and arms, drops of sweat across my eyebrows and down the back of my neck, hair stuck to my forehead and around my temples. All this as we stood motionless doing nothing.

"We've come to see the ruins," I told Ryan.

"Figured as much. That's the only reason anyone ever comes to Tikal." Ryan spilled coffee grounds on the jungle floor and swore. He removed another scoop in a careful and slow, if perhaps shaky, motion. He threw some wood on the burned embers of the old fire. The fire crackled and soon the smell of brewed coffee decorated the air.

Yvette put up our tent and we strung our hammocks. I was struck by the boldness of the jungle, much more remote and awesome and fearsome than any we'd seen so far. I began to realize why Ryan kept a shotgun against the tree next to his hammock. I had respect for the jungle. It scared me, though perhaps not as much as it once would have, what with hurricanes and Guatemalan militia. There was a part of me that now held fear in much less regard—a mad, crazy part of me that felt I could tell the world to shove it and it would obey. It was a nice thought, anyway.

The rest of the archeologists returned to the camp later in the day. There were eight in all, part of a team from Berkeley. They washed and rested in their hammocks until it was time for dinner. We went to the house of a Guatemalan family where we had a simple delicious meal of beans and rice and stewed chicken. Night arrived in all its black glory. Yellow halos of soft light glowed from kerosene lamps like melancholy fireflies.

In the morning, Ryan looked better and was full of chatter. The wonderful smell of brewed coffee again leached out of the pot and mixed with the morning mist. Warm slivers of sun poked through a hole in the leafy mantle above us. I talked to Ryan about the ruins and the temples, pressing him for as much information as I could. He seemed willing, even eager, to tell me what he knew. I wanted to gain his confidence since he alone had the key to all of Tikal.

One by one, Ryan's team came by for coffee. There was an attractive girl named Jill, a large woman, not fat but solidly built. She was funny and talkative and very friendly.

After breakfast, people gathered equipment and canteens and took off down one path or another. Ryan continued to tell us about the ruins,

"As best we can figure there are about three thousand buildings here in Tikal left by the Maya. In sixty years, we've uncovered about a dozen" When he said that, his right eyebrow shot up and he poked his head toward me as if he himself had been startled by his own incredible statement.

Ryan, Yvette, and I started into the jungle through a forest of green and purple. Pockets of mist sent the morning sunlight into a crazy frenzy. Steam rose from the ground, giving the trees a surreal forbidden look. Yvette looked at everything with great intensity, pointing out insects and butterflies and birds and parrots, listening to the voices of the jungle and calling back to them.

We arrived at an open area. It was perfectly maintained; even the grass seemed to have been trimmed close and smooth. Two giant temples—pyramids that rose above the top of the forest toward the blue sky—faced each other about two hundred yards apart. Mammoth chess pieces from some forgotten game of long ago. Each temple was made of massive carved stone blocks set perfectly in place.

"That's Temple One," Ryan explained, pointing to the taller of the two. "It's called the Temple of the Giant Jaguar because of the relief of a jaguar carved across it. And that's Temple Two, the Temple of the Masks. These were first discovered by a crazy English explorer named Alfred Percival Maudslay back in 1881. He uncovered Temple One with the help of a few Guatemalans. See up on top there? There's a vault, a chamber used by the Maya as an altar, and there are secret tunnels that lead down inside the temple. It's a complicated affair. Temple One is taller than a fourteen-story building."

We were standing in the Great Plaza of the city of old Tikal. This was the nerve-center of the Mayan civilization. Ryan told us he had work to do and pointed in the direction of where he'd be.

The plaza was spotless and beautiful. There was nothing in sight to bring any context of time to it. Yvette and I looked at the two temples and at the half dozen or so other nearby structures. The open tropical sun burned down. Yvette said she sensed the power of Tikal. I said I felt it as we walked into the courtyard with Ryan. Yvette lay on the ground over the smooth soft grass—spread-eagle on her stomach and then on her back with her eyes closed and her arms and legs outstretched. She opened her eyes. "There's so much power here, Alex. Energy is flowing in and out of this place. Strong energy. I can feel it zap through my body." She looked at the two temples. "We should go to the top of Temple One, up to the altar. The energy flows like this…." She pointed first to Temple Two. "It comes from far out in the universe through Temple Two and across the land here and then up through Temple One and out again. Temple Two is the receiver and Temple One is the transmitter. See that, Alex…see that? We found it." Yvette let out a wild yell and spun in crazy joy.

CHAPTER THIRTEEN

August 19, 1980 – Day 78

A steep narrow staircase rose up the front of Temple One. We climbed all hundred or so narrow steps, some not more than six inches deep, rising up at a sixty-degree angle. With nothing to hold onto, we climbed on all fours like two clumsy jungle primates. We reached a flat stone platform that formed the top of the pyramid. We could see across the jungle in every direction. It was a magnificent view and it was obvious the temple had been built precisely to allow this, to look out over the thick lawn of the treetops.

Five large steps led from the platform to the altar. We entered a chamber lit only by vague light that came in through the open doorway. The altar vault was cool and quiet, much like the inside of an old monastery.

Yvette rubbed her hand against the limestone, feeling its craggy-smooth surface. The ceiling of the altar chamber angled to a point at the apex of the pyramid.

I said, "I think this temple has much more power than the ones in Palenque. I feel strange…do you?"

Yvette pressed her body against the wall. She walked across

the platform where sacred ceremonies had been performed. She looked at me. "This place is so mysterious, Alex. There are loads of things going on as we stand here right now…this very minute."

"The ancient Maya are still here, aren't they?"

"They're all around. The spirit of the Maya never left."

As Yvette spoke, the light coming in through the altar door-way faded. We turned quickly and looked out and saw a sky full of thick pregnant clouds. From our rooftop vantage, every inch of the forest around Tikal was turning dark. A wave of hard rain was moving toward us. It was that time of day when rain sweeps in. There we were, hidden in the greatest of all Mayan sanctuaries where, in a few minutes, Nature and the universe would converge.

Yvette said we should sit by the altar and wait for the storm in contact with each other. We sat cross-legged, my hands resting on Yvette's shoulders, her hands on my thighs.

The jungle turned to night. The chamber was filled with dinful shadows. Yvette's face was a silvery silhouette. Rain began to pelt the temple. A hard passionate rain. In a flare of light, the altar chamber lit up bright and ghostly. A vicious clap of thunder seemed to shake the whole massive temple, to lift it off the ground like a little dime store toy. When this happened, I felt warmth flow between me and Yvette, sometimes into me, sometimes over to her. The air inside the chamber changed. It was charged—no longer just empty space. It had a presence and a soul and a spirit. A streak of light shot into the room, spinning and swirling in a vortex until it blasted up through the thick stone roof of the temple.

I held Yvette's arms as the storm spun around us. It seemed to be speaking to us in some odd way. The rain blew into the altar chamber. A warm, moist, tropical mist filled the room. All in all, it lasted for no more than five minutes, the way the rains come and go in the tropics. As abruptly as it arrived, it was gone and the chamber was lit by the soft light of a fresh sky.

What had happened in the altar chamber was unclear, yet I felt somehow cleansed. Everything, even Yvette, carried a new and wonderful beauty that I hadn't seen before. I felt as though my spirit had been to confession. I looked at Yvette, hair tousled and hanging in her face. She touched my cheek, and we laughed and laughed. It was strange and crazy.

We climbed down from the temple and walked through Tikal looking for the archeologists. Jill was working near a small structure that was nearly submerged in overgrowth. She was studying the inscriptions carved by the Maya onto large stones called stelae. The entire stone, nearly six feet tall, was a tapestry of symbols and figures. She told us her specialty as a Mayan archeologist was in deciphering their calendar and dates. She explained the arcane writings carved onto the stelae and told us about the fifty-two-year calendar the Maya used—how precise and exact it was.

"Down along here," Jill said, pointing to the stelae, "these symbols make up a set of numbers. In the ancient Mayan language it says, 1 Kinchiltun, 11 Calabtuns, 19 Pictuns, 9 Baktuns, 3 Katuns, 11 Tuns, and 2 Uinals. Collectively, they add up to 1,841,641,600 days, or about 5,320,004 years."

"Holy cow!" Yvette roared. "What happened five million years ago?"

"We don't know if it means something in the past. It could be referring to the future," Jill replied. "Either way, it meant something to the Maya. They were far more precise than we are—until we developed computers, I suppose. For example, they knew exactly how many days make up a year on Venus. In fact, they calculated this to the second decimal point. They knew that there are 583.92 days in one Venus year. In order to correct for the 0.92 day each year, they dropped eight days from the Venus calendar every three hundred years."

"Christ, this must have been one big Mayan observatory here at Tikal," I said, looking around.

"All the Mayan cities were partly used that way—Palenque, Chichen Itza, Tulum, Copan. The Maya knew a lot of stuff we may never know."

Jill taught us about the Mayan people, how they thought and what they believed. She seemed thrilled to be doing this. I suspected very few visitors ever came by Tikal, given what it took to get there.

The jungle heat scorched us like grease from a hot pan. We drank water from our canteens as we watched Jill work under a tarp stretched across poles to provide a little shade.

We returned to the camp. Jill and Yvette and I talked about the Maya during dinner at the home of the Guatemalans. We remained for a long time after the others had left. A kerosene lamp lit the night. Smoke from the hearth cured the air of mosquitoes and bugs. In the dark night we learned about the magic of Tikal.

We told Jill that when we were on top of Temple One, we were seized by the thunder and lightning of the afternoon storm.

"The lightning flashed inside the temple," Yvette said. "Big, bright streaks of light swirled around. It came into the temple. But that's not possible, is it?"

Jill listened, saying nothing. I wondered if she thought we were a bit crazy.

"We want to spend the night on top of Temple One," I said. "Is that possible? Would Ryan allow this? He seems to trust us."

"That's right, do you think Ryan will let us?" Yvette said.

"You'll have to ask him," Jill replied. "But if you're interested, I can take you inside a Temple, down into one of the chambers?" She told us we couldn't go to where the digs were taking place. They were strictly limited to the archeologists, but she could let us see the passageway. She said she was going inside Temple Four tomorrow with Francois, a Belgian archeologist who was part of Ryan's group.

Yvette nearly leaped to the sky.

Late that night, filled high with expectation, we returned to the camp.

Morning brought great hope. I felt wonderful and rested. Yvette, as usual, was a lightning bolt. She was so full of energy and excitement she could barely contain herself. The archeologists laughed at her. Even Francois, the serious Belgian, shook his head and broke into a smile.

We got permission from Ryan to go inside the temple with Jill and Francois. I didn't ask him about our desire to spend the night on top of Temple One. One thing at a time, I figured.

Jill and Francois and the two of us walked down a path to the Central Plaza, then farther on through the jungle for a half kilometer or so until we arrived at Temple Four. A massive looming structure still largely covered by the forest, the tallest pre-Columbian building in the new world, soared heavenward for more than twenty stories. We walked to the back of the temple to where an old rusted metal door had been put in place by the archeologists, replacing a rock slab that had originally sealed off the passage.

Francois unlocked the door and wedged a large rock against it to keep it from closing. The passage was dark and narrow. Francois said, "The floor is very uneven. You must watch every step."

We followed Francois into the tunnel, each holding a flashlight. Jill came after us. The tunnel, barely wide enough for one person and too short for the tall Belgian, angled upward. The walls were damp and chilly. We moved slowly ahead. When we arrived at the top of the passage, the tunnel veered to the left and started downward through a series of slim steps.

"Watch it. It's slippery in here. Be especially careful," Jill warned. We were deep inside the temple where not even a shred of light from the outside could penetrate. There was only pure perfect darkness and the faint glimmer from our flashlights. A bat flew past my head, scaring the hell out of me. Francois chuckled. "They live in here. They must know of openings we haven't found."

Deeper down into the belly of the temple we went. Up above I saw figures painted in blue and red carved on the walls. I asked what they meant. Jill said at one time all the temples at Tikal, inside and out, had been painted in bright colors. The jungle rain and the sun had scrubbed the buildings, all but for the insides. What a sight Tikal must have been, I thought, with its three thousand red and green and blue pieces set amid the green backdrop of the lush forest.

"What do the words say?" Yvette asked.

"It tells us this tunnel passage was built in about 700 AD." Francois pointed to a life-sized relief of a Mayan man wearing a headdress and big bulbous earrings. He had a staff in one hand and a spear in the other. "He was a prince," Francois said. "He's buried here somewhere, but we don't know where."

At the bottom of the descending tunnel the passage forked. One part led into a vault about ten feet square, the other half descended farther. Jill and Francois were scheduled to work there that day.

As we entered the vault, I felt a death-like coldness on my skin, an unfriendly feeling that Yvette sensed, too. Her hand gripped mine. Francois looked at us, as if studying our reactions.

"Wow, it's cold in here," I said.

"Actually, it's quite warm," Francois replied. He showed us a thermometer stuck to the wall by the archeologists. The temperature was in the low eighties.

"I feel very cold," Yvette said, rubbing her arms. "And this peculiar feeling. What is this place?"

"It's near the burial room for the king. His body is behind that wall. No one's ever gone in there, though," Francois said.

"Are you going to?" Yvette asked.

"There is a legend much like the ones of the Egyptian pyramids. The writing on the wall tells us the tomb is guarded by spirits that accompanied him after his death. To open the tomb would send the spirits back into the world. One is a spirit of famine, one is drought, one is for disease. We can't interpret the other."

Yvette got all worked up. "But it's real! Don't you feel it? Holy shit! You feel it, don't you, Alex? These spirits are real and powerful. They want us to stay out."

"Easy," I said, putting my arm around Yvette.

"Are you afraid to be here?" Francois asked.

Yvette calmed down. "No," she said. "I'm okay."

"Do you believe in Mayan spirits?" I asked Jill. "Do they exist?"

Jill shrugged.

Francois turned on a battery-powered lantern that filled the room with light. He told us his specialty was studying Mayan pottery and that most of the sacred temples had pieces of pottery that told a lot about Mayan life. The room was covered in carved writings and drawings along the walls and up across the ceiling. Elaborately carved reliefs of Mayans like the ones we'd seen on the way into the temple. There was an open vault on one side of the room. Francois worked in a small roped-off area, taking out pieces of clay pots that had been shattered by the recklessness of previous visitors.

Jill recorded what was written on the walls. It told about a king, high priest of the Maya. His death allowed him to pass into another life out in the universe. According to what it said, he could return to Earth using the temple. The bodies of two servants and two young maidens who had been sacrificed at his death to accompany him into the afterlife were buried also.

All morning, we watched Jill and Francois work. In the afternoon, we went outside and ate tortillas and cheese and mangos and papaya.

The day was clear and hot. We returned to the temple for several hours more. Toward the end of the day, Francois closed the chamber and we went to where Ryan was working. He was curious about our day at the ruins.

CHAPTER FOURTEEN

August 21, 1980 – Day 80

Tikal was every bit the euphoric drug I hoped it would be. We were getting to the day when we would meet the Maya face to face. But I was not sure I was ready for that. My unsettled thoughts of Stef and Nash in Belize haunted me. I missed Stef and worried about him, fearing he was now in some wretched Belizean jail with Nash the wild man—Dauphine long gone. I loved Yvette, and I loved being with her, but inside me there was a sad and sorrowful part that wouldn't stop aching. I hated the thought of giving up one person for another.

I told Yvette all these things in the hopes of purging myself of the gamma energy that seemed to be controlling me. We agreed to wait another day before going back to Temple One.

Sleep that night came in troubled spurts. The howler monkeys wailed all night. Their pitiful songs filled the dark forest—screams of terror in the thick air like cries of sacrifices from the top of Temple One. Yvette curled close to me in our hammock, but I didn't feel that sense of oneness I usually knew. I felt lost and uncertain and worried—Jesus in the Garden of Gethsemane. Finally, very late, I dropped into a dull sleep full of laconic dreams and grotesque creatures. In the morning it was good to awaken, to see the green jungle and the sun and the mist. And most of all to see Yvette.

We spent the day at camp. I slept off and on. We bathed in the rain during the midday downpour. In the afternoon when Ryan returned to the camp, he found us swinging lazily in the hammock. He asked if we were tiring of Tikal. "Seen enough?" he said, rinsing his face with water.

Yvette said, "We have a very special request. Alex and I want to spend the night on top of Temple One."

Ryan didn't answer.

I said. "We wondered if that would be all right."

Ryan walked toward our hammock, rubbing the top of his head with a towel. "Well, it's sort of against the rules, you know." His brow rolled into furrows. "Why do you want to do that?"

"We'll be leaving Tikal soon. It would be very special for us to…well, to—" I began to say, to be with the spirits of the Maya, but I merely continued, saying, "Everything is so terrific here. It would be spectacular to spend an entire night up on the temple. It's all so…I can't describe it…so mysterious to us."

"We came such a long way just to be here," Yvette implored, "Months by bus…through a hurricane, even."

Ryan putzed around, doing this and that. "People come through Tikal now and then. Not a lot of people, but some…visitors, travelers, Gringos like you. Someday I'm sure Tikal will be discovered…it will be part of the tourist spots for people to visit, like Machu Pichu, for example. People will be bussed in to see the ruins. The place will be overrun by people from everywhere." He winced. "Ah, that's all right…I suppose. But for now, it's just us. I'm the protector of Tikal, you see. Although most Guatemalans think of Tikal as a special place, a sacred place, the government doesn't do much to protect it. Lots of times I feel as though they don't really give a shit about it. If it gets destroyed, well that's just the way it is. Sounds crazy, huh? But then look how we Americans sometimes treat the Great Lakes or the ancient forests in California, or whatever. We're not much better. If you take something for granted, it gets abused and ruined. When I'm here, I watch out for Tikal. By now you've probably heard about the smugglers—the people who come in and take whole chunks of stelae and pieces of the temple back to sell in the States. They're ruthless bastards. They'll kill you in a minute. I don't keep this thing here just for the jaguar…." Ryan picked up the shotgun next to his hammock. "Or this either…." He pulled a fine old Colt 45 from his day pack. "It's the two-legged animals you have to watch out for...plus the jungle, of course."

Ryan talked on about all sorts of things. As he sat in his hammock across from us, you could see the many different people that made up this interesting and complex person. The intellect that was always there as he spoke and thought and listened. A certain, self-assured, non-competing sort of intellect. A rugged man with character of steel who could deal with the raw elements of Nature as well as her fine theories. I saw a gutsy man, bold and tough when needed, with a softer side that displayed humanness and compassion.

What he said made such good sense that there was nothing for us to say, so we just sat there, though our question had not been answered. Finally, he took from the things next to his hammock a bottle of tequila and three glasses. He handed one to Yvette and one to me. He poured tequila into each. "To a very special night in the jungles of Tikal. May you find the Maya." We downed the tequila. We had Ryan's permission to go to Temple One.

The sun was beginning to set when the rest of the archeologists returned to the camp. We ate our traditional dinner of beans, rice, and chicken.

After dinner we prepared to leave for Temple One. Ryan warned us to be extremely careful. "Going into the jungle at night is no game," he said. "Everything out there is looking for dinner. And quite frankly folks, the two of you are not much of a match for a six-foot cat. The smugglers usually don't come around when we're here, so I wouldn't anticipate problems from them. Best thing to do is go now before the sun is completely gone."

That was it. We took to the path that led to the Great Plaza. Yvette walked next to me, sure and tough and ready for anything. The sun was sinking fast. A blue darkness was spreading over the forest. Yvette pulled out her flashlight and panned the ground in front of us. The quilt of branches woven tight overhead stole what little light came from the moon and the stars.

"Where are you, Alex?" Yvette asked.

"Here next to you," I replied, touching her arm.

We were about halfway to the temple when we heard a sound from the bush behind us off to our right, something big slinking its way deftly through the leafy forest. Stalking us, it seemed. Yvette spun around and aimed her light into the blackness. "Do you hear that, Alex? Shhh! Listen...listen. What is it?" she whispered.

I saw nothing. We moved farther on; still, it seemed to be following us—moving fast when we did, stopping when we stopped.

"We have to get out of here," Yvette insisted. "Maybe it's a jaguar, like Ryan said. Quick, let's run as fast as we can."

"No!" I said. I held Yvette by the arm. I picked up a rock about the size of my palm and rolled it in my hand until I had a good grip as you do with a baseball. I snapped quickly around and pitched the rock into the jungle in the direction of the noise. It worked perfectly. Whatever it was, it fled into the thicket.

Soon, we arrived at Temple One.

Climbing the steps of the temple was a slow ordeal, but because the Central Plaza was free of foliage, the sky bloomed in a vast universe of flickering stars with a beautiful quarter moon. From the top of the temple, the jungle was like black lace. The sheen across the tops of the zapote trees reflected the moon's glow as across a pond of silvery water. The night was hot, but a faint breeze spun past us on our perch above the jungle.

We sat for a while watching the vast forest around us and talked quietly as if not to disturb that world, sharing our feelings and confirming our commitment to each other. Yvette went inside the dark soulful altar chamber to absorb the energy that it held. She listened to its mood, sensed its obtuse directives. We settled onto the altar floor. There it all started and all ended.

⋏

Once again, a vortex of light spun around us. I felt my soul thrashing through the air like a wisp of smoke. Floating, sailing, soaring. First through hollow blackness. A void so empty that it felt like death itself, yet I felt very much alive. Soon I was spinning and twirling in the void. A void that seemed infinite. I saw nothing but thick smoke that surrounded my soul. I raced through this like a strange, fast memory. Everything then changed and all about me I saw purple. Silky purple. For some reason, I knew this to be Time. The present and the past and the future all thrown together in one. My spirit was worried. I pushed through time—muddy and thick. Far in the distance, I saw an end to the Time. I hurried, wanting to get there. My soul hated Time.

There was a burst of light and I was soaring through the universe. I felt wonderful. Bright colors rushed past me and rubbed against my spirit. I moved euphorically through a sea of colors. Colors that turned to shades of red and orange and pink and then gradually to deep crimson and then a loud crack of thunder filled the air so loud it hurt my earless ears. I stopped moving and my spirit came to a rest. The red colors turned to soft blue and turquoise—like the friendly waters of the Caribbean. My journey was complete. With me there in the universe was Yvette. Our spirits had arrived together, perfectly and harmoniously.

A vague form greeted us. He told us he once lived at Tikal.

"We have brought you here," he said, "because of your search for meaning in life."

A second spirit appeared. He said he was a king named Coatecatl, whose tomb was here in Tikal.

I told him we were seeking the answers to the questions our

civilization couldn't give us. That we hoped to find the answers from others who might know.

Coatecatl said our people were like termites destroying the very home we inhabit. He said we were letting stupid people rule our lives, and stupid people have none of the answers to any of the questions. He said we were technologically strong but intellectually weak. There was still a chance for our civilization, he said, but we must relearn many things. "My people raised the power of the mind to a very advanced level," he said. "Your people can do the same."

We talked about many things. Other spirits appeared and vanished. Some looked like wolves, but were highly intelligent creatures from other parts of the universe. I wanted to reach Stef as I had done with Miles when I was in Palenque. I tried hard to find Stef's soul and I asked the spirits to help me. Yvette tried too, but it was useless. I was worried and guilty and now I was sure Stef was in some kind of trouble. Coatecatl said you can't reach every spirit, especially those that don't want to be reached. That made me worry even more.

The blue universe pulsed with spirits as our quest for knowledge continued. When it ended, we left the same way we had arrived. We soared back through red and orange and then through purple Time again, exiting in the year 1637. We sat in a room at a table in a shadow-filled Flemish tavern in the city of Amsterdam. Yvette and I were poor, ragged, simple people. We drank beer from large thick mugs. The room was gloomy and there was the smell of burning wood coming from a big hearth that stretched halfway across the wall. Yvette had a shawl over her shoulders. I wore a tattered jacket. My hands were those of a worker. Poor as we were, Yvette was beautiful.

We drank bitter beer and talked about the people in the room, this one and that. A man entered from the street through an oak doorway. With him came a blast of sharp air. He sat at our table. The tavernkeeper brought a large mug of beer that dripped thick brown foam over the rim. The man had a beard and steely eyes and hair that hung to his shoulders. He wore a Flemish cap dipped down along the side of his head. He wore a cape. We talked and laughed and then...and then in conversation I heard myself say, "Well, indeed, you are a very strange man, Rembrandt." And with that Yvette laughed. "Strange? Huh, he's not strange...just a little crazy." And Rembrandt laughed full and hard and his steely eyes shone like crystal.

I gave Rembrandt a shove and we laughed again. Rembrandt reached over and swung his arm around my neck the way Stef used to do, and, in that instant, I realized a purely cosmic thing. I realized that once, long ago, Stefan Kale was Rembrandt, and that I was once a Flemish plebe of no significance, and that Yvette was someone I loved even back then. The revelation of this turned my soul to ice.

Our spirits were lifted and soon we were soaring through the black void, sailing fast into the emptiness—cold and lifeless—until we returned to the light of the faint moony glow that covered Tikal.

We awoke sleepy from our journey. I looked about and saw morning beginning to bud over the jungle. A pale pink glory crept over the forest. The stars were still turned on far out in the universe from where we had just returned. I put my arm around Yvette and looked into her soft eyes. I felt love all around me. I had experienced something so good it frightened me.

We stood up and stretched our earthly bones, watching the day grow around us. As I looked across the jungle from the top of Temple One, I knew nothing would ever again be the same for me. I knew that what had happened was irrevocable and that the direction of my life had now somehow shifted. I did not know where this course I was on would lead, though I was sure that every purpose had been redefined, every need recalculated, every thought forever altered by my night on the top of Temple I. It was a feeling founded in the new understanding of my life, what it was and what it can be. I did not yet fully know where my life would take me, but there was no uncertainty that the course I was on had been laid out and charted.

We returned to the camp and found Ryan ready to leave for the ruins. The others had already left.

"Well, did you find it?" Ryan asked, filling his canteen.

"Find what?" I asked.

"Whatever you were looking for? Did you find it on top of the temple?"

I was unprepared to discuss our experience.

Yvette, in a rare change of attitude, said not a word. I answered, merely saying, "Yes, I think so…yes."

"It rained like hell last night, didn't it?" Ryan said.

Caught off guard, I replied, "Oh…oh yeah, uh-huh it did."

"A real hard rain. We don't usually get those at night this time of year," he said. "Did you stay dry?"

Yvette assured him we did. "Everything was fine."

Ryan packed up. "Well, take care." He slid off into the jungle to the west of us.

We were famished, so we went and bought breakfast from the Guatemalan family, who prepared a grand meal of eggs and black beans and tortillas. The morning was perky and sweet. The jungle was green and misty. Songbirds sang love songs. We ate breakfast quietly and each time I looked across at Yvette she smiled, holding the secret of Tikal inside her.

After breakfast Yvette said, "Alex, let's go out into the jungle today. What do you say? Let's go way back as far as we can, all alone. We'll be Adam and Eve in paradise. Okay? Just for the hell of it."

I looked at the glow in Yvette's eye and felt the electric excitement of her exotic idea. It would be a good companion to our heady discovery of the previous night. A chance to synthesize all the feelings that had educated our souls—alone in the jungle in harmony with Nature as we had been in harmony with the universe.

We brought only the things we needed, the bare essentials. Water, a compass, my knife, a blanket. No need for food because the jungle is an overstuffed pantry. We each took one of Ryan's machetes and headed down a path that led east from the camp.

It was a warm, lovely, glowing morning. The jungle was a ripe and verdant forest. The green colors appeared as cool shades of lime and blazing dark neon splotches. Finches and parrots and birds of all kinds buzzed and circled and darted over us on fast frenetic wings. They were good companions and perfect sentinels to any danger nearby. As long as they spoke, all was well.

The path narrowed to a single lane until soon it was necessary to carve away branches to get through. Walking and cutting, cutting and walking, we pushed slowly ahead.

"Oh, look, Alex!" Yvette said.

I turned and saw Yvette pointing with her machete to a gargantuan spider's web that gleamed in the sunlight, a web nearly five feet across. In the center, a yellow and black spider big as my fist hung upside down.

My spine chilled. "Let's go," I said. "I hate those things."

Yvette laughed. "They're sorta pretty."

We continued farther away from the camp, cutting as we went. A family of monkeys congregated above us, disturbed by our presence. They watched with nervous eyes as they nimbly sailed across the jungle ceiling from branch to branch. We pressed on slow but steady, stopping to see everything along the way. Near midday, we came to a small stream with clean shallow water and grassy banks. This would be our camp for the day.

"How far have we traveled?" Yvette asked.

"Quite a way," I calculated. "I'm not sure. It's hard to know exactly when everything looks the same."

We waded into water that came barely up to my waist. Yvette put her arm around me. My hands followed the smooth line of her body from her shoulders to where the water met her hips.

"It's so warm, so beautiful," Yvette said.

We got out and lay on the blanket to dry in the sun. I closed my eyes, feeling lazy. Yvette lay motionless next to me. Suddenly, she jumped and screamed. Above us, a snake as thick around as my bicep twisted across a branch, slithering slowly.

I held Yvette's arm. "It's okay," I said. "It won't harm us. Some kind of boa constrictor, I think. Just let it go on its way."

Yvette took my hand and put it on her chest over her heart. "Feel that?" she laughed. "It's beating like a bloody freight train." She lay on the blanket, keeping an eye on the snake until it crossed the water and vanished into the jungle.

"Maybe that was the devil," Yvette said. "If you're Adam and I'm Eve, then that must be the devil out here to tempt us." Yvette smiled. Her eyes were devilish and very tempting.

"Maybe it was. What if it was?" I toyed. "What could it tempt us to do out here, alone, by ourselves, disconnected from the world? Tell me, Eve, what could it tempt us to do?"

Yvette traced her finger across my eyebrows and down my nose and over my lips. "Oooh, I don't know, Adam. It could tempt us to...*sin*...I suppose."

And thus we did, and afterwards we fell asleep on the blanket. Hours later I awoke and looked around, momentarily lost. Yvette was gone. I was alone in the forest. I sprang to my feet and searched everywhere but saw no sign of her.

I called into the forest over and over again—still nothing. Fear of some horrible tragedy swelled inside me, and then I heard Yvette's voice off in the distance.

"Where are you, babe?" I called.

"Over here. Look behind you."

I turned and peered into the forest, cutting through it with my machete. "Where are you," I said again.

"Up here...look."

Yvette had climbed one of the banana palms. How she did this with a machete in her hand, I'll never know. She cut off a bundle of bananas, tossed them to me, tossed the machete down, and climbed to the ground. On the ground by the tree was a large papaya and a pineapple that she had gathered also.

"You scared me out of my wits," I told her.

"Sorry, love," she said with a kiss. "You were sleeping so peacefully; I wanted to surprise you with these."

We ate the fruit of Yvette's harvest. Little by little we were becoming adept at living in the jungle, at finding food among the plethora of plant life, spotting all the interesting and beautiful and dangerous parts of the forest. Yvette, especially, saw everything. She heard every sound and perceived every creature. She had a natural instinct for this strange and foreboding place.

Yvette said, "Think how far we are from the rest of the world. Imagine if we were totally alone on the planet, as if it was just the two of us, the two of us and no one else left in the whole world. Not a single other person. It's a brand-new planet, and we are the first two humans here…us and the animals. The spiders and the snakes and the monkeys, and everything else. What kind of planet should it be? We can make it any kind we want."

"I want there to be just ordinary people with no hatred and no wars and no weapons. And if we have governments, I don't want them to be like the ones we have today—mortally insane, designed to ruin the world."

"If the world ended right now, we might be the only people to survive. Then we could start everything all over…brand new."

"Most governments are crazy, either a little or a lot. I believe that now more than ever. Like Coatecatl said, we give stupid people the right to rule our lives and—"

When I mentioned Coatecatl, my thoughts stopped. I had inadvertently brought us back to our night on Temple One.

Yvette looked at me. Her face became serious, as if waiting for what I would say next. I stopped talking about the world and its crazed governments. I sat quietly eating a piece of papaya. In the silence of the noisy jungle, we waited for each other to speak.

Then, without much thought, I said, "Yvette…I'm lost. I'm very lost. And I'm confused. I don't know anymore where I'm going or where I've been. A part of me has gone back to being a child. I'm…I'm bewildered about myself, about everything. And yet, I know my life is moving forward, going *somewhere*." I pointed into the jungle as if there were a road that I was destined to follow.

Yvette listened to every word. But the more I spoke, the more my words began to sound ridiculous and stupid. As quickly as they came from my lips, their sense seemed to vanish. I thought this must be confusing for Yvette…Yvette who never troubled with the things that scratched at my brain, cutting through it like an icy saw.

She was a person gifted with a special vision of life, and most of that vision existed in the present. She never stared into the past or gaped at the future. There was something enviable about that kind of vision, particularly when you believe you don't have any of it yourself. People like me, people who spend their life thinking about the future, miss the present. But perhaps now I was changing a little, not very much probably, but a little. Being around Yvette

helped. She was the first person in my life that made me understand the present. All my life so far, the questions had been, "What
are your plans, Alex?" and "What will you do now?" and "What
about your future, Alex?" But now those questions seemed lifeless
as a mannequin, and each day I learned a little more from Yvette
and a little more from the Gringo Trail.

"Are you frightened by what happened last night?" Yvette
asked.

"Somewhat," I replied. "How do we know what we thought
happened really happened? If it did, what did it mean? And if it
didn't happen, then what was it we experienced?"

"You're too much of a scientist, Alex. You worry about a lot
of unnecessary things. How do we know we're really here, now,
right now, this minute.... How do we know that?"

"I just accept it," I said. "I don't worry about that."

"Because you believe it's real, and you believe it's happening
now, don't you?"

"Of course I do. I see it happening and I feel it. That's not the
same, though."

"Oh, yes it is." Yvette leaped to her feet. "See the forest,
touch it, feel it, look at the colors, hear the birds and the monkeys,
the toucan up there—right there, see it all yellow and black? And
the snake that came by. Those things happened. And last night,
didn't we see the colors of the universe, and didn't we wade
through Time and feel its coldness, and then the warmth of being
with Coatecatl, and the smoky room at the inn with Rembrandt?
Didn't you smell the smoke from the fire and taste the beer? Was
that different from this?"

I thought for a while. Yvette was right, it was no different. She had focused on the very essence of my question.

I said, "The difference is that here in the forest I can believe what I see because these things are like other things I've seen before. Though I've never seen a wild toucan, or a big snake, or an anteater, I know they exist. Or at least I already believe they exist even before I see them, so when I encounter them, my mind accepts their existence. My mind is aware of them before my eyes have witnessed them, or my nose has smelled them, or my ears have heard them."

That statement brought me to the nucleus of the eclectic experience on Temple One.

"But before last night, my mind could not prepare—except in some type of fantasy—for what we experienced. So I...so when it happened, even though part of me was ready for it, I pushed it away, calling it a dream, or a hallucination, or something." I stared straight into Yvette's eyes. "You believe it, don't you? You believe all of what happened last night. Without any trouble you accept it. But it's not that easy for me. I mean, I want to believe, but it's not that easy. I don't have your vision of things. That's why I'm confused and why at times I'm lost. I'm lost inside my own head, tangled in my own thoughts, stuck in mud thick as Time itself. Sometimes I feel a little crazy because I feel like I'm doing things that are sort of forbidden. I mean, no one ever said to me, 'Alex, go off to the Mayan jungles and search for the universe and for its meaning.' But why didn't anyone tell me that? Isn't that worth doing? Isn't that what people are really trying to do back at the university?" I sighed deeply and lay back on the blanket and fixed my eyes onto the toucan in the tree above us. Its big awkward bill looked strangely out of proportion to the rest of its body.

The jungle was now engorged with steamy heat. The sun had passed over the sky and was falling back into the forest. I tried to digest what we'd discussed. I ate some fruit passively. Yvette said it was getting late, so we gathered our things and retreated back toward the camp.

It was a tough walk. The sun was slipping fast. The more we hurried, the more we stumbled and tripped. The forest was filling with cryptic shadows that grabbed at us, and all I could think about was Ryan's advice about not going into the jungle at night. Coming out took longer than going in due to a couple of wrong turns. By the time we returned to camp, the forest was a soft shade of purple and the black night was just around the corner.

Ryan was waiting for us. As we walked in, he gave us a piece of his mind for almost getting trapped in the jungle at night. We apologized for making him worry, admitting it was foolish of us for not being more careful.

Later I told Jill I felt bad about upsetting Ryan. She said it was nothing. She said Ryan likes to be "Papa" to his little tribe of people here in the rough-tough jungle. Sure enough, Jill's interpretation turned out to be correct because soon Ryan came by and talked to us as if nothing had happened. I told Ryan we would be leaving in the morning; it was time for us to go on. We thanked him for his hospitality. I knew in my heart that someday I would return to Tikal, and I knew that until then a part of me would remain in the misty hot jungles caught in its magic. And most of all

I knew that some of the answers were still in Tikal—hidden, buried. Obscure, yes, but not lost.

CHAPTER FIFTEEN

August 23, 1980 – Day 82

We left Tikal in the morning. Said goodbye to the group and to the Guatemalan couple who cooked our meals, strapped our packs to our backs, and took off for Flores with fresh canteens of water. I never looked back because I wanted to remember the huge Mayan relics as they were, fused in my memory.

At Flores, we made plans to leave immediately for Guatemala City. It had been ten days since we had anything that could be considered a bath or shower. We went to one of the small hotels; for fifty cents, the manager let us use a shower.

We boarded a bus for Guatemala City. A sorrowful bus packed with Guatemalans four to a seat—seats made for two people. This was the most elemental, the most basic, bus of all—a homemade bus! An engine, a drive train, axles and wheels, to which everything else had been constructed of wooden planks—the sides and the window frames. Sheets of steel and tin had been nailed to make the roof.

People stood in the aisle. Men rode on top of the bus with the bags and boxes and baskets. This would be a deadly long trip, first through the dangerous jungle of eastern Guatemala, then south to

Honduras, and finally up to the mountains and highlands of western Guatemala. Under the very best conditions, it would take twenty-four hours, if everything went right—otherwise longer. We bought plenty of food to get us through.

Yvette looked at the inside of the bus, "Alex, I don't think I can ride in there, packed in with no air. Do you know what this will be like in a few hours? These buses don't stop and when people have to go to the toilet, they just use a can or whatever they have. It's like a concentration camp in there."

Yvette climbed the ladder on the back of the bus. "Give me the packs," she said, "It's fine up here."

I handed her the packs and climbed the ladder. The Guatemalan men looked suspiciously at us. Gringos up on top of their bus—a woman, no less! Women never ride on top of the bus. They sit inside with the children and the old men. The roof, when necessary, was for the young virile men. They would keep a close eye on the evil jungle. And yet, here on top with them was the most Gringo-looking woman they had ever seen. No one said a word, though, and soon we rattled out of Flores down into the forest.

"Buenos dias," Yvette said, as she settled down between a large bag of rice and a box of mangos. She thanked the men for letting us ride on top.

The bus slid deep into the jungle. The afternoon heat was tempered by a big breeze as wind blew across us. We rode on for six or seven hours without stop. Dusk arrived, putting some of the jungle to sleep and bringing some of it to life. Nighttime smothered the jungle. The Guatemalans on top of the bus opened a large tarp and stretched it across, making a kind of tent. From there, we could see the trees as they slithered behind us.

Around midnight, we arrived at Honduras near a coastal town called Puerto Barrios over by the Caribbean. The bus stopped and we ate at a darkly lit roadside restaurant.

Soon again, our one-bus caravan searched out the jungle. It was good, even comfortable, up on top. Somewhere, while rumbling through the thick wet tropical night, we fell asleep.

Late into the night, the bus rolled to a stop. A flat tire, I thought—something like that. I leaned over the side. The bus had emptied. People loitered aimlessly about. I looked inside the dust-covered window of the bus and saw a few people standing close to a dim lantern. I was unable to tell what was happening. Suddenly, there was the piercing cry of a woman. Seconds later, the sweet cry of a baby using its lungs for the first time filled the air. The midwife cuddled the new life in her arms. A woman leaned out the window and called, "Es un niño!" Everyone cheered. The child's father knelt down and made a sign of the cross and looked to the sky and thanked God and Jesus and Joseph and Mary and everyone he could think of.

Minutes later, the bus was filled and we were off. A new life had come to our little bus, unimportant to the world perhaps but just as in the very jungle through which we passed, life went on no matter who was there to witness it. Life as good as any in New York or Moscow, Tokyo or Washington. Seeing that, I realized that there is no such thing as a better life or better people. There are only people more arrogant and people more humble. Life is the same. And it's a pretty simple thing really, this thing life—not such a big deal unless you're so caught up in it that you never actually witness seeing it.

Yvette was so moved by what had happened she couldn't sleep. Morning rose from behind the bus in a pale light over a purple jungle. Dust from the road churned up in our wake and mixed with a misty dawn that soon gave way to a hot morning. A savage afternoon fried us like eggs on the tin roof of the bus.

Late in the afternoon, we emerged from the jungle onto the low grassy plains and then slowly climbed a mountain range, around and around and up. The grass was green and thick. Crops grew from the side of the mountain. We passed villages inhabited by Guatemalan natives dressed in colorful skirts and shawls.

Up into the mountains, three thousand, four thousand, five thousand feet. The air was thin and cool. We had to put on our ponchos and hide under the tarp to keep warm.

We had been in the tropics for so long our skin had changed. It was not prepared for the cool weather. The bus rolled on. In time, the dirt road opened into a two-lane paved highway and we sailed along at forty or fifty miles an hour, which seemed like ninety from the top of the shaky bus. Yvette hung on tight to anything around her, afraid that one good bump would catapult her off the back of the bus. The Guatemalans laughed and made jokes each time we hit a bump, gesturing with their hands as if she was going to shoot into the air like a rocket.

Around midnight it started to rain. A cool, drizzly, gloomy rain that forced us to huddle under the tarp and made it difficult to sleep. In the early morning we arrived in Guatemala City. We went to the nearest hotel where we fell into a lifeless sleep.

Part Three

Rethinking

CHAPTER ONE

August 24, 1980 – Day 83

Guatemala City was a big place that held little interest for us. The rain stopped in the afternoon and the day turned bright and clear. You might think that after a bus ride like the one of the previous day, no one of reasonable sanity would consider getting on yet another one. But we did.

The Pan American Highway weaves through the mountains of western Guatemala—a concrete ribbon through lofty green peaks. The bus purred strong and healthy and its big wheels hummed against the highway like the big buses of northern Mexico.

The highlands of Guatemala were a spectacular sight. Green and lush and peaceful. There was a serenity that didn't exist in the Yucatan or even on lazy Caye Caulker. Those places were infused with tropical heat. The highlands of Guatemala were as tranquil as a New Hampshire farm. The towns were small and perfect, each with a zocalo, a market, a cathedral, and restaurants. The people were descendants of the very Maya who once lived in Tikal and Tulum and Palenque, the brothers and sisters of Coatecatl who had left the jungles for the green mountains. I wondered if they still had that special gift of knowledge and learning that Coatecatl possessed, and I wondered if someday these people would again share their knowledge with us. Or was the knowledge gone forever, as Coatecatl had suggested? Were these people permanently lost in a world in which their ancient customs were lost as well? Once kings and queens and princes now pawns to the powers of the world—to their own government. Yet I saw nobility in their strong faces. In the deep, clear, rust-colored eyes. Nobility that ran through their veins.

From high in the mountains, the world looked like a pretty good place just as it did when we climbed the mountain in Trinidad's van. Looking down, everything seemed achievable and unchallenging. The astronauts left us with that impression when they viewed Earth from their far-off orbit.

Yvette stared out the window, hypnotized by the green mountains. She rested her head against the glass as our big bus rolled through the steep hills. "It's so beautiful, Alex."

I thought about Stef and I missed him. He should be here with us, next to the window making music with his camera. Drunk on a celluloid high. This was his place. It waited for him, to capture it as Monet or Matisse might have done—the sliver of clouds, the mist, the green and yellow mountains, Indians and oxen and donkeys. All in its pure and simple glory. And then he would reload his camera—talking wildly the whole time, raving, full of that madness that overtook his soul at those moments. He would laugh and Yvette would fill up with that same crazy madness and that same exhilaration. And, of course, to see them like that would make me explode with joy. I knew Stef should be here. But he wasn't. I stared out the window—sad and sick. I didn't see all the beauty that Yvette saw.

We rode all morning, stopping once at a village called Chichicastenango. A place with a wonderful market filled with thick wool ponchos and serapes and fine jewelry.

In the afternoon, the bus turned off the highway onto a dirt road carved into the side of the mountain. The road coiled up past four thousand feet. We climbed through clouds that hung around us like white cushions, there to catch us when we slid off the road and down the mountain, which I was sure would happen at any second. Up higher, then down the back side. Out before us, off in the distance, was a smooth lake, blue as a new pair of jeans.

Yvette looked out the window, her hands flattened onto the glass. "It's Lake Atitlan!" she said. "This must be the city of Panajachel. *Wow!*"

I saw a lake with three towering volcanoes perfectly positioned around it that stretched far into the sky. Around the tip of each was a halo of thin clouds. This was the lake we had heard about as far back as Isla Mujeres. The bottomless lake that sits a mile in the sky.

The village of Panajachel was a postcard. One small road led in and out. There were cafés, a few restaurants, and an old hacienda that served as the local pension. We got a room. I bought a bottle of cold water and lay back on the clean white sheets.

Yvette saw the weary sadness in my eyes. She buried her head against my chest. "Is it my fault, Alex? Tell me the truth—please tell me. It is my fault, isn't it?"

"Is what your fault?" I answered, trying to be naive.

She rubbed her hand across my forehead. "You know what I mean. It's my fault about Stef, isn't it?"

I stared at the ceiling, at the blistered paint that lined the old adobe. "It's not your fault, Yvette. I never thought that for a minute."

"Alex Moreau, I love you more than the whole world and everything in it. I'd trade anything for you.... I'd...I'd give up my sight for you. I'd die for you. I'll die without you. Oh, please, believe me. Please believe me." Yvette's eyes swelled with tears.

"I'm sad," I said. "Maybe I should go back to Baltimore and pick up where I left off. See if Markham can put in a good word with the people at MIT, try to get my fellowship back. I never could have imagined before I left all of the things I would see and do. The experiences, the beauty, the tragedies. And you, of course. Meeting you. Meeting someone as spectacular as you. But I wonder, sometimes now I wonder, what did I learn that I didn't already know? I thought traveling down here would change my life. Now, I wonder...well—"

"But it's been good, Alex. I know it has. You're better for having been here. We both are."

"Right out there, not far away, is the Pan American Highway. It's everything that the Gringo Trail was and more because it will take us far, far south. All the way down to the end of South America. To go down the highway, what would that be like? For in here, I mean." I tapped my chest. "For our soul...our soul? For who we are? Can we continue to travel, spending almost nothing, living without a worry in the world?"

"Yes, yes, yes we can!" Yvette insisted immediately. "We

can!"

"I wish that were true," I replied.

"It is true!"

"Sooner or later we will have to turn around and walk back into the world…the real world. Not this world where tomorrow never arrives."

"Who knows, maybe tomorrow will arrive and we will end up in a very special place we never knew existed and we will want to stay there forever. Stay, live, work. It could happen…it could."

I shook my head.

"It could happen, Alex. It *will* happen. I always believed that the hidden agenda for my trip, the real reason I was here, was to find what I couldn't get out of life before I left."

"It's nice to think so, but that's a storybook life. Those things never occur in the real world. We don't just stumble haphazardly onto Valhalla…Nirvana. Think about it, if that were the case, we wouldn't be marching down the road, riding in beat-up old buses and trains searching for something that probably doesn't exist. We tricked ourselves into believing that today, tomorrow, the day after maybe, we will arrive at that special sacred place."

I looked at Yvette and saw remorse in her eyes. And yet I knew that for both of us, every experience we had had on the Trail had been transformative, had permanently etched its lasting effect into the very fiber of who we were. And that, I knew, was a good thing.

I said, "I thought sooner or later we would find Stef again somewhere on the Trail."

Yvette pulled close to me. I felt the soft skin of her back. We held each other tight and made love and then slept until the morning's call from the rooster.

CHAPTER TWO

August 25, 1980 – Day 84

It rained the next day. A drizzly, foggy, London kind of rain. I was happy for this because I wanted to be close to Yvette. More and more I was fed by a craving to be with her always. From the small window in our room, we could see the tips of the volcanoes guarding the edges of Lake Atitlan. The smell of mountain rain filled the air. A Guatemalan villager paddled across the lake in a fine smooth line under draping clouds and a silvery mist. In the afternoon, we had dinner at one of the restaurants. We talked and laughed and Yvette was more herself again. I was beginning to feel better too.

We inspected the volcanoes and went to the lake and stared into the deep water where there were supposed to be vast amounts of gold and gems thrown in centuries ago by the Indians in sacrifice to the gods. Divers have tried to recover the treasures but the lake is too deep and too dark. It gave up nothing.

In the afternoon, we wandered through the market. Yvette bought a big warm poncho. As we walked back to the pension, I subconsciously uttered, "I think I should be back in Baltimore. It's nearly September, and if I'm going back, well—" The words stuck in the air.

Yvette grabbed my hand tightly but didn't answer.

Later, we climbed aboard a bus heading back to Mexico. The border between Mexico and Guatemala is an empty desolate forest similar to the one we passed through when we entered Guatemala from Belize. The sun was already setting. We went across the checkpoints, but this time we refused to make camp at the border, afraid of encountering another petty squabble between two countries.

We set out on foot surrounded by sullen gray hills and a dark sky, leaving behind the suture line that connects Guatemala to Mexico. We were in the state of Chiapas—rugged land unaltered by the hand of man. We hadn't walked far when a station wagon carrying a Mexican couple whizzed past us. It stopped and backed up. A door swung open inviting us in. We graciously accepted.

We spent the night in a small town a short distance up the road. Early in the morning we were on a bus cruising through the mountains toward the city of Tuxtla. We decided to go past Tuxtla and straight on to Oaxaca.

I stretched a map on my lap. From where we were, Oaxaca looked like a short distance, but the mountains outside the bus said it would be a slow ride even in a good bus. At midday, we stopped at a roadside restaurant and ate fruit and bread and had coffee made from beans grown in the hills around us.

The bus engine roared and soon we were swerving through the high mountains of south Mexico, the Sierra Madre del Sur. The mountain highway was narrow and dangerous, cut into the edge of the hills without a railing or even a shoulder to keep us from falling off the edge of the world. The drivers of these buses had nerves of steel, like the boxers who come out of the barrios of Latin America. Driving the road was a game of chance waged between the buses and cars and trucks. Vehicles racing down the mountain at full tilt like some out of control roller coaster. Then, going up, cars and trucks two abreast nearly blocking the road, creeping along, air horn blazing, unable to avoid anything heading down. All this on the edge of disaster set thousands of feet above the world. *Somewhere down in the thick forest below must lay the rotten guts of countless wrecked vehicles,* I thought.

We continued to climb at a sharp angle, the bus grinding hard, purring like a mountain lion. Suddenly, the engines stopped and the bus coasted to a halt. I looked ahead and saw a line of traffic going to the next bend in the road. I was sure this must be one of the disasters I had envisioned. We moved ahead slowly, everyone in the bus stretched to see what had happened. Yvette knelt on the seat.

"What is it?" I asked.

"A bunch of people standing in the road."

Then I heard a man say, "Es un toro."

"There's a bull in the road," Yvette said.

"A live one?"

"No, a dead one."

We pulled closer. As we neared the scene, everyone on the bus pushed to one side near the windows. Indeed, there was a bull, a big one. Killed by a truck, I suppose. Three men hovered over it with knives, slicing it from horn to tail in one massive bloody mess, butchering it piece by piece. Mexican women in black shawls stood nearby and stacked the cut meat on newspaper. One bull—no matter how it died—can fill many tortillas with tasty meat. Up above, circling in the sky, buzzards waited for their chance.

The bus swung around the bull, gunned its engine, and took off into the green hills. Late in the afternoon, we passed the city of Tuxtla. Around eight o'clock, the sun vanished to our left as we started out of the mountains. For two hours we came down slowly and gradually until we emerged into an open valley that was spread before us like a big serape. Our bus, longing for the straight clear highway, raced across the open land like a young stallion. Far in the distance we could see Oaxaca, the old provincial city known for its cathedrals and markets and cafés. We had heard about a place to stay in Oaxaca from two Canadians we had met in Guatemala. When we arrived at the city, we went to a campground not far from the zocalo. It was late. The streets were dark and mysterious.

The homes of Oaxaca were Spanish-style places with French doors and lacey curtains and fine wrought iron. We walked through the city, stopping now and then to rest. At the campground, a Mexican man named Perez let us in the gate and showed us where we could stay. For a small fee we could rent a cabana or, for less, we could string a hammock.

In the daylight the next morning, the campground looked like many of the odd places we'd seen along the Trail. I saw tents that had been up for months. People looked as strange as Yvette once did when I first saw her back in Villahermosa. I realized I was one of them. Hair to my shoulders, headband to keep hair from my face, tanned skin, faded shirt. Muscles tight from months of carrying my world on my back.

CHAPTER THREE

September 3, 1980 – Day 93

We stayed at the camp for a week. We had moved into a small wonderful cabana just behind the hut where Perez and his wife guarded the entrance to our vast estate.

Perez, being a Oaxacan Indian, spoke very little Spanish. He was always friendly, always walking through the camp sweeping the clay dirt with a homemade broom—always with a smile on his face.

The zocalo in Oaxaca has no comparison in all of Latin America. It is closed in on four sides by old buildings with fine elegant architecture and beautiful wrought-iron balconies. Street cafés with snappy waiters that would have made Nash proud delivered delicious food to the tables.

We had coffee in the cool morning sun and talked about the beauty of the plaza stuffed with flowers and palms, shoeshine stands, and ice cream vendors. Pretty ladies in cotton dresses passed through the zocalo. Oaxaca is every bit the essence of Old Mexico. We spent the morning at the market and in the afternoon we found a small restaurant on a charming street off the zocalo. We ate lunch and had a bottle of wine. The restaurant was dark and cool. Its patrons were from the upper tier of Oaxacan life, all smartly dressed—cool and keen looking. The women were elegant and thin. A man wearing a rumpled white shirt and a cowboy hat came into the restaurant carrying an old worn Spanish guitar. He walked between the tables playing songs with fingers that flipped across the strings in a transparent blur, releasing sweet chords out into the room. He sang sad ballads of endless love, hopeless love, forgotten love. His eyes were filled with all that sad love. The songs sprung from deep within his heart.

We left the restaurant and weaved tipsy through the narrow streets of Oaxaca. The city was winding down to its evening pace. We returned to our cabana and fell fast asleep.

Voices…I opened my eyes. Late and pitch black. I could hear Perez talking to one of the Germans at the camp. We had met him that morning. He had told us he was a painter who had come to Mexico to work and that he had been in Oaxaca for several months. I remember him describing the sight of the soft afternoon light as it shined on the zocalo in a yellow hue. "Finer than in all of Paris," he'd told me. His name was Hans. He was very intense.

I heard Hans screaming at Perez. From his speech, I could tell Hans was very, very drunk. The night held almost no light except for a soft moon glow. I saw Hans stagger towards Perez and swear at him. He pushed Perez, causing him to trip and fall. Perez got up and, in a rage, charged the German, who deflected Perez. Perez's wife came out of their hut, hands waving and yelling, telling the two to stop it. This all happened a few feet from us. Hans put his head down and charged at Perez like a bull, knocking him down. He smashed his fist into Perez's face. Perez pushed Hans away and climbed free of the German. In the shadow, I saw Perez's wife grab a three-foot machete, its gleaming blade honed like a razor. She handed it to Perez, who sprung to his feet while Hans was still on his knees. Perez held the big blade with both hands and raised it high overhead and sent it whistling down. I saw the flash of the blade. Hans rolled to one side, holding his hand in the air instinctively to protect himself. There was a savage scream like a pig in a slaughterhouse. Hans rolled in circles on the ground. I leaped from my hammock and tackled Perez and grabbed the machete. Hans continued to roll on the ground. I ran over to him and saw blood spurt like black oil from his hand. I grabbed his arm and saw that the blade had caught him squarely between the third finger and the little finger and had taken the little finger clean off, through the bone and the tendon and the flesh and everything, completely severed. Blood continued to squirt from his hand; Hans groaned in agony. I worried that in all his drunkenness he might go into shock. I ripped off my shirt and wrapped it around his hand tight as I could.

The rest of the camp had come out carrying lights and lanterns. Hans continued to bleed profusely. We changed the dressing several times, but the bleeding continued. One of the camp residents got his car. We pushed Hans inside and took him to a clinic—he was losing blood fast.

CHAPTER FOUR

September 4, 1980 – Day 94

In the morning the camp was very quiet. Everyone talked about the incident of the night before. Somehow, we all felt strangely responsible for what had happened. Some of the people said Hans was a little crazy when he was drunk, but not enough to deserve that. Ironically, the camp was owned by a doctor in Oaxaca. When he heard what had happened, he quickly fired Perez. By noon, Perez was gone and a new groundskeeper was in the front hut.

Hans returned from the clinic in the afternoon, his hand wrapped to the elbow. He was more furious than ever because it was his painting hand that had taken the blow.

"I can't work now," he raved. "That mother fucker ruined my source of income. I'll have to peddle everything I have to the damn tourists in the zocalo. All of this for nothing. If I ever see Perez again, I'll kill the bastard."

That you could believe.

It was far too sorrowful for us to stay any longer in Oaxaca, so we packed our things and left to find a bus going north. In the depot, I stared at the board deciding what to do. Buses were going everywhere: north to Mexico City and Guadalajara, east to Puebla and Vera Cruz and the Yucatan. Then I saw one lone bus destined for San Miguel de Allende. I grabbed Yvette and raced across the station just as the bus for San Miguel was backing out. Yvette yelled to the driver and banged on the door. I didn't give a damn how crowded the bus was, I wanted to be on it. The driver stopped and opened the door.

All afternoon we passed through a desert that looked very familiar—hot, dry, dusty. It smelled like the ones of northern Mexico.

Late that night the bus closed in on Mexico City—that same tin can city and same diesel-fume air. It took two hours to get in and out. Near morning we arrived in San Miguel. Almost nothing in my life felt as wonderful as stepping off the bus onto the cobbled street of Miguel. Still tired and beat down from the bus ride, we walked to the plaza and checked into a hotel.

The next day we had coffee in the café by the zocalo that Stef and I used to go to. I told Yvette, again, what a magic place San Miguel was. We spent the day searching the city. I hoped to find Andy or Miles or anyone from before. We went to Miles's house, but no one was there. They had all gone, I supposed, all left San Miguel just as we had done. San Miguel now wasn't quite the same.

I stared out the French doors from our hotel room and watched the afternoon sun paint the zocalo, much as Hans had described for the one in Oaxaca. Yvette came out of the shower. She dried off and stood next to me, smelling clean and wonderful. She kissed my shoulder. "I still love it here, just the way it is. I'm happy to be here, Alex."

I smiled and kissed her and ran my hands through her wet hair.

By eight o'clock I was antsy. "Let's go out. I need a beer."

We got dressed and walked into the zocalo where vendors were cooking fish and chicken on little fires. I put my arm around Yvette's shoulder. We walked up Cinco de Mayo and entered the door to Las Tortugas. It was dark and smoky inside. We couldn't see much, so we stood for a second in the entrance. I looked around, then in the darkness I heard someone shout, "Alex! Yvette! Holy Christ, it's you!"

I looked over and saw Stef leap to his feet. He pushed his way through people and chairs and threw his arms around me. We spun in a circle, clutching each other. He grabbed Yvette and lifted both of us off the ground in a burst of joy. "I missed you two," he roared. "Oh, shit, I missed you two bastards!"

Yvette broke down and cried big wet tears of joy, laughing all the time. I looked at Stef. He looked beautiful—healthy and tanned and wonderful. As I looked at him, I felt a great burden vanish from my soul. Happiness flooded my body.

In the corner of Tortugas, I saw Andy and Miles and Chloe and Gerry the painter, all just as they'd been when we were there months ago. God, it was wonderful. Andy came over. We went back and sat at the table and I introduced Yvette to everyone. We ordered drinks for everyone and Chloe sent for a bottle of tequila. Andy toasted to us all. Then we had a round for the Gringo Trail— that wild, insane, wonderful place.

Stef told us everything that had happened to him. It was obvious Dauphine wasn't with him and it was obvious he was happy she wasn't.

"Nash went to Guatemala sometime after you did," he said. "I came back to Mexico with Dauphine, but at the border the Belizeans threw me in jail. Dauphine hung around for a few hours, then got worried and split and left my ass there to die. The jail was a rotten little room not far from the border checkpoint. I was in a cell made of cinderblocks with two windows each about ten inches by ten inches and a bare dirt floor. One of the windows had a screen on it, but the other was open. At night mosquitoes came in in droves. During the day the temperature went up to a hundred and ten or so because the building was out in the sun with no shade. There was an old drunk Belizean in there with me, and a Swedish guy who was busted at the border for having dope. He was in a heap of trouble and he knew it. On the second day, they came and took him off to the main jail at Belmopan. He looked real worried when he left. It scared the shit out of me to see him go."

Stef washed down his words with beer and went on. "I didn't know how long I'd be in that jail, they forget about you real quick. Twice a day they send over a bowl of rice and some fish and fried platanos and they leave a big tin can of muddy water scooped from the river to drink. God knows what diseases are cooking inside me now. Then, after three days, one of the Belizeans came to the jail and said, 'You are free-e-e to go. I suggest you go *ba-a-ah*-ck to Mexico.' I grabbed my things and split. I ran into Dauphine up in the Yucatan. It was all I could to keep from killing her—if I hadn't just got out of jail I probably would have. Then I just looked at her pitiful little self and decided she wasn't worth it. But I told her if I ever saw her again I might not be so generous."

I told Stef and the others about our trip through Guatemala and back to Mexico. Being back in San Miguel was a wonderful feeling. There is such joy in hoping for something and then just when you think there is no more hope, when you're about to give up and you've resigned yourself to what seems like a certain sad reality, a small miracle happens and your hopes come true. That's what it was like being back in San Miguel.

All this happiness filled Yvette, too—not surprising being the sponge for emotions she is—happiness and sadness and joy and sorrow, each one in its own time until every gram of her flesh burns with these one by one. She was happy to be reunited here at Las Tortugas, twice as happy knowing how I felt about it all. Knowing that everyone was back together, all but Nash. Nash was gone now, but people like Nash never really leave you. They continue to exist in your life in some peculiar subliminal way. At times that evening I could almost see Nash sitting with us at Las Tortugas, leaning back in his chair, cigarette cocked in his mouth, lips curled, eyes glanced away. Wherever he was that night, he was also with us at Las Tortugas.

I told Miles about everything I had learned from the Maya, and thanked him for what he had taught me. I explained that I had decided to return to Baltimore and see about my fellowship at MIT. My mind had been cleansed—all the litter that once prevented me from thinking was gone. My brain had been rewired. Its frayed neurons had been replaced. Now, every pampered new thought delighted me just as in those early days when I was sitting in Markham's office, toying vicariously with science's big questions, hearing the trajectories of genius that came from his flashing mind as they bounced around his office while I sat there, listening, learning, trying to keep up, tossing in a weak and feeble idea of my own. The Gringo Trail had relit that energy in me.

We drank another round of beer and had more shots of tequila. I watched Stef sitting between Andy and Chloe. I could feel the electricity that sparked through his body. I talked to Miles and told him all about Yvette and her magic and the Maya and their magic and about theta energy and I thanked Miles for bringing all that magic into my life. We stayed at Las Tortugas until everyone had left and the bartender was cleaning up and the piano player had gone. We walked out into the wonderful night air of San Miguel—the city I once knew and now had rediscovered.

CHAPTER FIVE

September 11, 1980 – Day 101

I Remained in San Miguel much longer than I should have. I was very broke, but I had just enough to get to Baltimore if I used my thumb and nothing else. The crew in San Miguel wanted to buy a ticket for me, but I refused unconditionally.

Stef planned to stay and work with Andy. In a few months, Andy would be going to New York to see his publisher. I had a chance to read his manuscript; I could tell it was exceptional. Stef would return north with Andy and Chloe when they came up. We decided Yvette would stay in San Miguel until I could get back to Baltimore to square things with Dr. Markham, and with Maureen, if need be. Then, she would come north to Baltimore so we could be together. That was sealed in love.

Andy located a truck going to the US border with a load of fruit. The driver agreed to take me that far, after which my thumb would get me home.

On a sunny morning outside San Miguel, a big diesel waited impatiently. The engine roared and Hernando, the driver, said, "Vamanos, amigo."

I gave a hug to everyone. I could barely stand to leave. I climbed into the cabin of the truck. Hernando shoved the clutch in, jammed in the gears, gave three torrential blasts of the air horn, and we rumbled down the road. From the window I watched San Miguel shrink behind me. In front of us was the desert, and off in the distance those mountains—always those mountains. The truck took on speed. Soon we were barreling through the vast empty land of central Mexico.

My mind seeped with thoughts of the trip from its very pre-beginnings. Thoughts of Elvira the waitress, and Ozzie the used car salesman, and gentle Jose Ramirez. Harvey and his apartment in San Miguel. Trinidad and the sweet mountains of the east. Hector the Inspector and the jungle train ride. The black-eyed women of Vera Cruz. There was Sal the conch diver. Kind dead Michael and sweet Coca and little Francisco. The Belizeans and Mrs. Reeves and Lou and Len. Dauphine, damn Dauphine. The Carters and the wild Guatemalan militia. There was Ryan and Jill and Francois and the whole bunch at Tikal. And then, recently, Perez and Hans. And of course, Andy and Chloe, and Miles the magic poet, and Gerry the painter. Nash, 'focking' Nash. Yvette—beautiful, wild, wonderful Yvette. And always, always, always Stefan Kale.

Made in the USA
Monee, IL
23 June 2020